T0064119

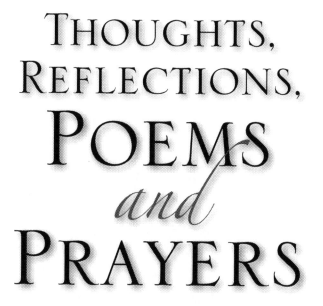

THOUGHTS, REFLECTIONS, POEMS *and* PRAYERS

My Soul in Print

SAMUEL C. WILLIAMS

PARTRIDGE

A Penguin Random House Company

Copyright © 2014 by Samuel C. Williams.

ISBN: Softcover   978-1-4828-9593-3
          Ebook   978-1-4828-9265-9

All rights reserved. No part of this book may be used or reproduced by any means, graphic, electronic, or mechanical, including photocopying, recording, taping or by any information storage retrieval system without the written permission of the publisher except in the case of brief quotations embodied in critical articles and reviews.

Because of the dynamic nature of the Internet, any web addresses or links contained in this book may have changed since publication and may no longer be valid. The views expressed in this work are solely those of the author and do not necessarily reflect the views of the publisher, and the publisher hereby disclaims any responsibility for them.

To order additional copies of this book, contact
Toll Free 800 101 2657 (Singapore)
Toll Free 1 800 81 7340 (Malaysia)
orders.singapore@partridgepublishing.com

www.partridgepublishing.com/singapore

Foreword

I never imagined in my wildest dream that I would someday morph into a writer of any sort. I entered the Jefferson County High School (Louisville, GA) in 1969. The next year we were forced to integrate. Therefore, in 1970 I became a reluctant member of the Wadley High School student body. I quickly learned that integration for blacks was not the same as integration for whites in small town USA. White parents, to avoid having their children attend school with black students, quickly (literally over the summer months) erected independent "academies" (which are still in existence and operation today) and enforced racial codes as the primary basis for admission. These all-white (totally illegal) academies took with them many of the white students and teachers who were unaware yet un-accepting of their darker peers and colleagues.

However, one of my WHS teachers who had spent years at the school prior to the arrival of black students decided to remain there, ostensibly as an instructor, until the time of her fast approaching retirement. She was my English teacher. But, she never taught us English. As a matter of fact, she never taught us anything. For three consecutive years, as a college bound student, I was assigned to her classes and was never taught a single thing. Albeit, upon entering Paine College in Augusta, Georgia in 1973, I was fortunate enough to encounter Dr. Joyce Cherry as my first college English professor. Dr. Cherry was a no-nonsense instructor who took English far too seriously for me. Then one day she sent her assistant to my dormitory to get me for an unannounced conference with her. During the conference she made me aware that she was highly impressed with my style and ability to analyze and write.

I was floored because I knew that based upon my background I should not have had the requisite academic foundation to develop the skills of which she so forcefully and unwaveringly insisted that I possessed. Notwithstanding she held fast to her assessment of my skills and informed me that she had made a major and difficult decision to change her standards for me as a student in her class. Of course I argued that she could not change the standard for a single student in a class, but would have to change the (already unbelievably difficult) standards for the entire class. She assured me that she could and she did. She forced me to read, write, analyze, think and see as I had never been "taught" before. (She was convinced that I had a natural gift and that it was her mission to bring it out of me. I was content to allow it to remain exactly where it was.) I completed a total of three classes under Dr. Cherry before graduating with a BA degree in English. My plans had completely changed and so had my life. I'd gone from believing I was going to become an architect to knowing that I could become a serious writer at any point that I chose to sit down and apply myself to the task. Well, many schools, many years, many experiences, many degrees and many memories later, I've finally decide to tap into that "gift" to which Dr. Cherry had introduced me eons earlier. Having completed and published other works, I am now currently working on four other separate projects and two novels. Admittedly,

I am eternally grateful to Dr. Cherry and have tried to reproduce in the lives of my students, the very same impact she inspired in mine. I thank her immensely as she never once concerned herself with what I came to college not knowing. Rather, she focused on what she knew I needed to know in order to get to where my "gift" could take me. Over the years, this has become and remains my teaching philosophy as well. Thank God for the persons of wisdom whom He puts along our paths to usher us into our destinations.

About the Author

Samuel Williams is the author of more than twenty plays and musicals and ten different books. The author currently lives and teaches in Yokosuka, Japan where he also doubles as a minister of the gospel and a high school girls basketball coach. Williams is a former Army officer and photojournalist. He is the husband of his college sweetheart, Sharleen Williams. The couple has been married for nearly 40 years and are the proud parents of one son, Samuel IV and one daughter, Shaudalynn. The proud couple also have two beautiful granddaughters, LeAndra and Jordyn Williams.

Williams attended the George Washington Carver Elementary School and the Wadley High School in his tiny hometown of Wadley, GA. Upon graduating from WHS Williams attended Paine College in Augusta, GA from 1973-1977 where he earned a BA degree in English. After graduating PC in 1977 Williams entered the U.S. Army and served his country both as an enlisted and commissioned soldier for the next several years. Prior to leaving active duty service Williams received an MPA degree from Golden Gate University in 1991. He has since received his Ed.S degree and is now pursuing his doctorate.

Williams is now in his twentieth year as an educator. During this timeframe he has taught at the middle and high school and college levels and has held virtually all leadership positions associated with each of these levels. He concedes that the progress as well as the process of education has been as important to his growth and development as a person, teacher and mentor as it has to those whom he has taught.

Williams is a wonderful inspirational speaker whose exceptional oratory skills are often sought out for religious, athletic and various other special events. Individuals and/or groups interested in contacting Williams for such an engagement should do so at <u>manifestnow1@yahoo.com</u>.

Special Acknowledgements

There are many special people who are definitely deserving of recognition for their roles, unwavering support, inspiration and motivation for this project. I would like to express my sincere gratitude to some of them. Invariably, I will inadvertently omit someone; however, I ask that such an omission be construed as an attribute of age and not that of a callous heart.

GOD: I sincerely thank You for Your motivation, inspiration, insight and "gifting" needed to complete this task.

SHARLEEN (MY WIFE): Thank you for being that constant support system. You have been there every step of the way, and for that I owe you an unpayable debt of gratitude. I love you.

SAMUEL AND SHUNDALYNN (MY CHILDREN): I thank God so much for each of you. It is because both of you have constantly reminded me of my love for writing and have fervently encouraged me to take up my pen and do what God has gifted me to do, that I am again pursuing my calling and gift. You two are the treasures in my life. I love you both.

RUBY WILLIAMS (MY MOTHER): You never allow me to forget that not only am I the only son in the family, but that I am also a special son to God. You have always been there to support and encourage me. Thank you. I love you.

GERALDINE, BEVELYN, JOANNE, PATRICIA, SONYA (MY SISTERS): Having you all is like having five more mothers in my life. No one could ask for a more supportive family cast than you have been for me. Thank you all. I love you.

Contents

Just Let Me Do What I Can   1

Let Me Have Peace   4

Always Pray   8

Call Him Up   10

So You Will Know   13

When I Am No More   15

Gone Home   17

A Letter to God   19

Sunshine in the Storm   23

In Touch   25

Satan Never Quits   27

Miracle at School   29

A Teacher's Prayer   36

I Gave You Me   44

The Heart of Man   58

A Prayer for Bible Teachers   60

Our Daily Bread   63

The Power of Your Belief   66

A Faithful Spirit   68

The Peace of God   71

My Hurt   73

To the Women I Love   79

The Anatomy of a Female   81

Mama, Can We Talk?   84

Mother's Day 1995   90

My Spiritual Mother   93

My Ebony Mother   96

Ebony Queen   99

A Mother's Love   102

Happy Birthday, Mom   104

Who's My Mother?   107

To Grandmom   109

Grandma   111

Encouragement to a Spiritual Sister   112

Random Thoughts   118

I Love Getting High on God's Drugs   124

Remembering You   125

On Being One   128

Looking For Me   129

Love Is   135

In the Morning   137

Making a Champion   139

Success   143

Letting Go   145

My Prayer   148

Say Thank You   150

The Lord Is   151

A Christmas Prayer   153

Despair   157

A Morning Meditation   158

A Sunday Morning Prayer   162

Why Come We Be Like We Do?   167

Warrior's Prayer   172

In Touch   174

The Duties of Love   176

3 . . . 2 . . . 1 . . . Eternity   178

Never Apart   181

Inspired Love   182

Surrendering of Process   183

If I Held Just This Day   185

Thank You   188

Insatiable Love   190

Me   192

A Talk With Daddy   194

In Anticipation   199

Quitting   201

Race and God   202

The Rainbow Station   204

Rising   206

Second Guessing God   208

Stand!   213

Good Morning, Fear   219

Yes, Jesus Loves Me   224

A Moment With Jesus   227

(Un)Secret Lovers   228

Goodbye, Best Friend   230

Good Morning, Jesus,   231

Giving Up to God   235

These Feelings I Have   238

Dreams   241

As the Cocoon Opens   244

My Daddy   249

Contemplations   253

Come Forth   260

The Call to Freedom   261

We Yet Scribe   263

Beauty   270

A Prayer for Dad   271

A Simple Prayer to Begin Your Day   273

Believing God's Word and Prayer   284

Purge Me That I May Be Holy   289

Hold Fast to Your Confidence   291

This Day With You   293

Amen to Your Word, Decrees and Promises   295

THE WRITINGS IN THIS BOOK APPEAR IN NO
SPECIFIC ORDER OR SEQUENCE. RATHER, THEY ARE
SIMPLY A COMPILATION OF VARIOUS WORKS THAT
I HAVE AMASSED OVER THE YEARS. I HAVE SUB-
TITLED SEVERAL OF THEM IN ORDER TO PROVIDE
THE READER WITH INSIGHT INTO THEIR IMPETUS.
I PRAY THAT YOU WILL FIND SEVERAL OF THEM
THAT WILL SPEAK DIRECTLY TO YOUR SOUL.

Just Let Me Do What I Can

(Allow god to minister in your life through
the gifts and obedience of others)

Just let me do what I can.
I can never be all.
I can never do all.
I will never know all.
But I can be, do, and know that which I am, I
    will, and I can.
So please, just let me do what I can.

Just let me do what I can.
While I can never feel your pain
And while I can never see through your eyes,
Nor give ears to your world of sound,
I can still empathize, behold, and listen.
So please, just let me do what I can.

Just let me do what I can.

I will never tread a path carved just for you.

I will never become the person you were created to be.

I will never sing with your voice or shed a single one of your tears.

Yet, I too must walk my own path, hum my own tune, become my own person, and cry my own tears.

But for you . . . I am willing to do what I can.

Just let me do what I can.

I cannot create your memories

Nor can I bring you joy or give you peace.

I cannot be the dew on your morning grass

Or the sun rays that snake a path through the clouds in your life.

But I can be in your memories, share a smile, speak words of compassion, and welcome the arrival of each new day.

So please . . . just let me do what I can.

If it's little . . . just let me do it.

If it's much . . . just let me do it.

If it's often . . . just let me do it.

It it's seldom . . . just let me do it.

If it's external . . . just let me do it.

If it's internal . . . just let me do it.

If it's permanent . . . just let me do it.

If it's only for the moment . . . just let me do it.

Please . . . just let me do what I can. With *God* as my guide, *love* as my inspiration,
and joy as my motivation, won't you please . . .
just let me do what I can?

Let Me Have Peace

(Know god, know peace. No god, no peace)

If I have nothing else, let me have peace
  So that I may talk with my Lord
Let me have peace
  That I may focus on his goodness and grace
Let me have peace
  That I may see God in you and beauty even in
    despair
Let me have peace
  So that I can hear his voice in the whispering
    winds
Let me have peace
  So that I can wash my face in the raindrops of
    his tears
Let me have peace
  That I might admire his divinely spoken
    firmament

Let me have peace

  That I might hide his word in my heart

Let me have peace

  That I might not only be loved but show love
    as well

Let me have peace

  That I might see me in the misfortune of
    others

Let me have peace

  That I might learn to lie confidently in the
    arms of Christ

Let me have peace

  That I might learn to beg of him to experience
    a closer relationship

Let me have peace

  That I might learn upon every occasion to
    borrow from the powerful wisdom of his
    Word

Let me have peace

  That my soul might learn to steal away and
    seclude myself in his presence

Let me have peace
    That I might become a junkie on God's LSD
        (love, salvation and deliverance)
Let me have peace
    That I may be consumed in God's glory
Let me have peace
    That I may be empowered by his grace
Let me have peace
    That I may be inextricably confined by
        incessant forgiving
Let me have peace
    That I may follow him wherever he leads.
Let me have peace
    That I may seek to be perfect, just as my
        Father in heaven is perfect

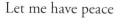

Let me have peace

  That I may taste of him and know that he is
    good

Let me have peace

  That I may operate in the divine powers and
    knowledge of my redemption and boldly say so

Let me have peace

  In my soul . . . peace in my heart . . . peace in
    my mind . . . peace in my ways . . . peace
    in my speech . . . peace until the end of my
    days.

If I have nothing else at all, please, let me have
  peace.

Always Pray

(Believers should pray at all times)

There will come times when attacks are many
And God himself seems distant and
 unconcerned
Go through what you may, dear child,
But never turn your back on prayer

Situations will rise and friends will fall
Family will dessert and pain will remain
Go through what you may, dear child,
But never turn your back on prayer

Confusion will abound and envy will destroy
Lies will hurt and deceit will devastate
Go through what you may, dear child,
But never turn your back on prayer

Poverty will befall and despair will accompany
Frustration will reign and desperation will seek
    to conquer
Go through what you may, dear child,
But never turn your back on prayer

The bread of heaven is plentiful and the joy is
    everlasting
The peace is without bounds and the love is
    omnipresent
Go through what you may, dear child,
But never turn your back on prayer

Call Him Up

(He's just a prayer away)

Something went terribly wrong in my life
   yesterday
No matter how hard I tried to overcome it,
   something else just got in my way

Regardless of my good intentions, my words were
   always wrong
My thoughts were totally vexed and feelings were
   unusually strong

Suddenly I found myself in the dogfight of my
   young spiritual life
But instantly the Word reminded me "Your
   adversary is the author of all strife"

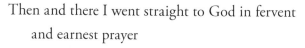

Then and there I went straight to God in fervent
and earnest prayer
And in the twinkling of an eye His empowering
grace was right there

Coursing my veins and renewing my mind
Reassuring my spirit man that He's in total
control at all times

"Cast your burdens upon Me," He said, "and I
will set you free
You have no need to fight Satan yourself. All you
need do is to call upon Me"

So I gave it up—my problem—and turned it
    over completely into His hand
Satan whispered to my mind, "You know you
    can't win the battle; you're just a man"

God replied, "That, Deceiver, is quite true. He is
    but flesh-and-blood man
But I, Jehovah the Almighty, am his battle-ax,
    his protection and his battle plan"

Without confrontation, battle, or even a slight
    discourse, Satan fled and my soul was free
And oh how I thank God for stepping in and
    winning the battle for me

So You Will Know

(A compelling love)

My child, my children

I laugh with you because my heart knows the joy
you are yet to feel

I touch you because your wounds I seek to heal

I hold you because your dreams I desire to make
real

I pray for you because your agony I ask God to
repeal

I counsel you because your soul I wish to be pure

I chastise you because I seek your best thoughts
and holiest demure

I cry with you because your disappointments I
know for sure

I encourage you to inspire in you the faith it
takes to endure

My child, I love you because this our Father
would have me to do

For how could I love our Lord if I did not first
love you?

When I Am No More

(My hope in christ)

When all my days are over and done and I have
answered the call of both burden and fun
Will I be able to say in my heart I know a good
race for the kingdom I have run

When all my days are over and done and I can
no longer impact the young on their final
outcome
Will I hear my Savior's sacred decree, "Well done
my good and faithful one, well done"

When all my days are over and done and I can
no longer admire God's setting sun
Will I meet Jesus in Paradise with my new life
having just begun

When all my days are over and done and I
have to lie down and forever more hold my
tongue
Will I then sing in the angelic choir or maybe
beat the heavenly drums

When all my days are over and done will heaven
hold for me countless rewards or none
Will Jesus know me not and reject my face or
will He thank me for the course I've run

Gone Home

(Good-bye to a blessed friend)

I should be as lucky as you
To have the privilege of being with God always
To live in the presence of the Omnipotent One
To feast at the welcome table
To praise and never get tired
To rejoice with loved ones long since departed
To laugh with Moses
To walk with Abraham
To hug Mary
To shout with Paul and Silas
To enlist in Joshua's army
To be in heaven with God
I should be as lucky as you.

I should be as lucky as you

To sing with the angels in the heavenly choir

To know today what the unseen tomorrow holds

To know nothing of evil and all about righteousness

To know peace that surpasses understanding and love that is unconditional

To finally greet St. Peter at the pearly gates

To hear God say, "Well done my good and faithful servant. Come unto me and rest."

To have known and to have served God and now to see Him face to face for eternity

I should be as lucky as you.

No! I pray. I shall be as blessed as you.

A Letter to God

(A fervent desire to acknowledge
You in all of my ways)

Any Street

Any City/State

Any Day

Dear God,

Today is no holiday, birthday, anniversary, or special event, other than it's another day that I am Yours and another day that You have kept me clear of the attacks of Satan. And since I have a free moment, I thought I'd use it to write You this thank you note.

All day long, You've comforted me, escorted me, guided me, protected me, and provided for me, and never once did You levy a charge for Your divine services. At sunrise, through the chirping of the birds, You woke me and greeted me with brilliant sunshine and pure thoughts. You talked with me as I prepared for my day and walk with me as I began it.

You kept me during trying times and guided me around Satan's pitfalls. You fed my body with your love and guidance while You fed my soul with endless servings of Your Holy Spirit. I saw my fellow man's behavior, but You looked deeper and saw his heart. I heard his words. You saw his thoughts. At time I fought to change his mind, You, however, changed his spirit.

Your vanguard has surrounded me. Your armor has protected me. Your word has made me sure. So now I can, by Your power and authority, take on the fiery darts and arrows Satan slings my way. I can walk the straight and narrow with confidence. I can live by Your commandments and bury myself in Your Word. Not because I am great, powerful, or omnipotent, but simply because I am Yours and You keep and strengthen me through all things.

My time is up and now I must return to work; I'll be back soon because I've decided to spend every waking moment possible getting to know You, emulating You, and pleasing You.

And so I've taken this first opportunity of the day to say "Master, I love You, I need You, I trust You, and I believe in You and the full integrity of Your holiness and Your Word. I pray that You will continue to keep me in Your midst always.

In love and admiration

Your child,

Sunshine in the Storm

(To receive the rewards of the crown, we must
first bear the weight of the cross)

When the skies of life begin to cloud
And the straightway seems more narrow and
harder to walk
That's when the spiritual sunshine in my life
rises
That's when I'm silent so that I can hear God
talk

When the tears race down my face like
waterfalls
And my trials come quicker than my solutions
That's when I go to God in faithful, fervent
prayer
That's when He reminds me, "I am your eternal
resolution"

When I have to stand all alone and watch the
world go by
And those I thought cared for me have
abandoned my trust and love
That's when I fall back on the promise of Jesus
my Christ
And am reminded that my hope rests only in
Him above

So now, when rages of persecution power their
way into my life
And it seems corruption and sin threaten to do
my soul harm
I will never give up, doubt, fret, or fear
Because with Christ, I've got sunshine in the
midst of my storm

In Touch

(God wishes to commune with us just as
we long to commune with Him)

Lord, as long as I stay in touch with You
It's so easy to know what You'd have me to do
I have no need to ponder, doubt, fret, or fear
For Your guidance is always so immediate and
clear

You guard my thoughts and control my mind
You monitor my speech and are there all the
time
You keep a smile spread across my face
You comfort me always with Your reassuring
grace

You protect my body and keep my soul
You fight my battles while your hand I hold
You're the keeper of my destiny and the overseer
    of my life
Lord, I don't know where I'd be were it not for
    your son Jesus Christ

One thing's for sure I've come to know
And I will boldly state it wherever I go
The longer I stay in touch with You
The happier I am that You're in touch with me too

Satan Never Quits

(Like robots, demons do not take breaks,
vacations, or time-outs)

When the sounds of the day have passed
And the stillness of peace escorts in the night,
That is when my soul best talks with You
That is when faith becomes my sight

When the drudgery of life finally stops to rest
And the battles of the day are truced for recess,
That is when my soul best talks with You
That is when my spirit is at rest

When the pains of life are reduced and calm

And disappointments have all past with the fallen
day

That is when my soul seems closest to You;

That is when my heart finds the perfect prayers
to pray

But never a time does Satan halt his attacks on
me

And never will he cease his diabolical and
incessant quests

That is why You have made my heart to know,
dear God,

That to remain Your child I must *always* be on
guard and at my best

Miracle at School

(A student is used by God to draw another)

Hey, check it out. Did I tell you what someone
    said to me today?
Some boy—I don't know his name or why he
    was even passing my way.
But still I was game so I took the time to hear
    what Dude had to say.

I was there at school, just chilling and trying
    hard to be incognito
When this big burly dude walked by and stepped
    right smack on my toe!
Truth is my flesh immediately wanted to tell him
    where I felt like he should go.
But I understood that the brother couldn't see
    my foot for picking his fro.

Then he looked down on my desk and saw I was
reading the Word
And (he) said the strangest thing to me I'd ever,
ever heard.

"Check it, that ain't nothing but mess. Why you
bother reading that silly crap?
If you wanna hear a real word," the brother
claimed, "check out this gansta rap!"

"Allite. Bring it on!" I said, "You've got a deal my
friend.
I'll listen to your rap if you'll agree to read what
God says about sin."

Dude hesitated. Thought about it. Pondered over
it a minute or so.
But I was patient with him because I knew it was
his his-hop image he was afraid to let go.

"Allite! Allite!" he finally roared. "That's hip. I'm
    game. That's cool!
I'll read your Bible, and you can listen to my
    jams, but tomorrow bring my CD back to
    school."

"Word," I agreed. "I'll be here bright and early
    tomorrow a.m.
There was no doubt in my mind I was going to
    see a change in him."

I kept my word and listened to the demons of
    hell speak to his soul through the lyrics of
    his CD,
And Lord was I happy I was prayed up before
    hand or they would have also spoken to me.

But I went before God and held my brother up in
prayer, refusing to giving the devil any kind
of victory

If this young brother can't pray for himself, Lord,
then accept this prayer on his behalf from
me.

His heart has been hardened, his eyes closed to
your awesome and miraculous deeds;

His soul is drunk with Satan's wine, and his
heart contains the corruption of the deceiver's
seed.

He has no idea what he's doing or what's going
on with him in the area of spiritual warfare

He doesn't know the consequences the devil
is bringing into his life are far beyond
compare.

But my prayer was answered. I was his
  intercessor. I stood in his gap.
And by way of a vision, I could see God's Word
  open and sitting upon his lap.

And for the first time, he saw love and knew
  forgiveness and came in the presence of God
  himself
He felt the anointing, experienced fellowship,
  and was reborn before he left.

I arrived at school early the next morning—
  energetic, excited, and ready to go
But the brother had beaten me to homeroom,
  and yes, he was still picking his fro.

I walked up to him and dropped his CD hard,
  flat on his desk.
"Hey!" he shouted. "I'm trying to read the Word
  here! Go sit down. Don't be such a pest!"

"You mean you like it? You understand it? You're really into God's Word and not gansta rap?"

"Are you crazy? I'm into the good stuff now. And take that CD off my desk. I don't want that crap!"

"But just yesterday . . . that's what you were saying about the Word."

"Yeah. You're right. But yesterday this time my soul had never heard."

"Heard? Heard what? What did you hear as you read the Bible last night?"

"It's not so much of what I heard as it is what I saw that had been hidden from my sight.

"Now all I could do was praise and thank God
        for what he'd done through little tiny me.
His anointing had spoken to a sinner, opened his
        eyes, and eternally set him free."

You know, it's so, so funny how God works his
        will through us, by us, and in spite of us too;
I guess if we just move ourselves out the way,
        then the Holy Ghost will perform that which
        He was sent to do.

But I just thought I'd share that with you—kind
        of a testimony
Of how God, to establish His kingdom, used
        even little old me.

A Teacher's Prayer

(A prayer for the school, the students,
the staff, the administrators, the families,
the community, and the teachers)

Father God, with a pure heart and willing and contrite spirit, I come prostrate before Your divine throne this morning for the purpose of fellowshipping with You, Your mercy, Your love, Your grace, Your compassion and with all that You are.

I acknowledge my weak, decrepit, and vulnerable state as a flesh-and-blood, mortal, imperfect human being. But I also acknowledge that by Your divine process of selection, You have chosen to bless me, endow me, appoint me, empower me, commission me, and send me forth on behalf of Your kingdom. Therefore, I recognize that in me, there is no condemnation whatsoever when I walk after the things and ways of the Spirit and not after the pride of life, the lust of the flesh or the things and ways of this world.

I know Your peace because I am not condemned. I know Your love because I understand that in spite of my weaknesses, I yet am neither lost nor cast away. I know Your grace, mercy, and love and am not condemned by the judgments of man. And because I am not, I know that whatsoever thing I ask according to and in compliance with Your Holy will, You shall hear and grant unto me according to not only You will and my petition, but also according to Your divine abundance in glory. I know it is Your Fatherly pleasure to give to all of Your children every good thing the kingdom has to offer us. I know that because of Your great love for us,

You will not withhold any good thing from us. I know that Your thoughts toward us are always good and with a cheerful and expectant end. I know that You wish that I should prosper in life just as my soul prospers in You.

I know that no good thing will You withhold from me. I know that You will open up the windows of heavens and pour me out a blessing that I won't have room to receive. I know that You are the God of more than enough. I know that You will make blessings to abound and to overtake us. I know that I will be blessed coming and blessed going, blessed in the city and blessed in the fields, and blessed in my deeds and blessed in my speech. I know that you will withhold the attacks of the devourer just for my sake. I know that Your mercy and justice will be with me always.

I bless You, God, just for You being You and for what You are in our lives. I thank You for being You even when I was unlearned and unappreciative for what and who You are. I bless You from the very center and deepest part of my soul. I acknowledge You in my heart and glorify You with the fruit of my lips. I vow to be only faithful and unafraid unto death and to make You to forever be the God of my entirety. I bond with You in spirit and in truth, and I enter into covenant with You this day to be not just a bondsman, a servant, a child, or an ambassador, but even a friend to You, the kingdom, and Your holy statues and laws. Truly Your ways are holy and perfect always.

God, I pray that You will grant me Your wisdom in loving, considering, caring, counseling, modeling, and encouraging students today. Teach me first, and then, Father, teach them through me. Please do not allow me to respond to the tactics of the evil one through the medium of my flesh, my own mind, or my natural understanding. Touch each unlearned and unconditioned heart as it crosses the threshold of entrance into this facility today. Shed Your love abroad through these very vessels, which today are turned away from your compassion and love. And let me only see the You that is in them and not just the lack of You that is in them. Keep them in Your love and care. I pray that You will cultivate an intimate relationship with their sprits and that even the most reprobate of them will be convinced, convicted and converted to you.

Let me, through them, see just how far You have brought me, and because You have, I know You still can and that You still do and that You still will deliver the souls of those who truly believe and receive Your word in their hearts. I recognize that I have been entrusted with the imparting of wisdom and enlightenment into these vessels, Your future spokesmen and representatives for the Kingdom, and this charge I do not take likely.

I thank You for every member of this small society called my educational team. I thank You and pray for the school's administrators, custodians, cooks, staff, parents, and students and every home and entity makeup of various neighborhoods from which they come and that You have charged me with positively and divinely influencing and ultimately changing. I pray for every member of the board of education, as well as every security officer assigned to ensure the safety of this institution.

I now see Your heavenly provided net of protection and security, peace, power, and wisdom descending upon this very school. I now see futures being positively altered and broken hearts and spirits being restored. I now see and thank You for the divinely orchestrated success in every area of endeavor. I decree this supplication to be Your will, and I submit it in total confidence because You have told me that I can have whatsoever thing I ask of you as long as I ask them in total, unwavering, steadfast faith, confidence, and belief and since I have honored and obeyed Your word and have done as You have prescribed unto me. I have a blood-bought, Word-backed right to have expectations of Your intervening, corrective, and securing powers.

And now I lay this petition at the foot of Your throne and refuse to see, believe, speak, or receive anything other than the manifestation of Your perfect will in this matter because I know the God whom I serve and petition. Now unto Him who is able to keep me in perfect peace and from falling and is able to give unto me more than I can ask, think, or even imagine, according to the power that works within me, I humbly submit this supplication of exhortation and praise. And I further ask, Father, that you will release a special angelic influence of peace and serenity upon every student parent, administrator, and community leader this day. With confidence, authority, joy and faith we humbly submit this prayer in the matchless name of Jesus our Christ, amen.

I Gave You Me

(The Gift of God Within You)

(In order to fully understand this poem, you must first let your mind go to the place and time that each of us must inevitably face someday. The place is heaven; the time is . . . well, that's the point of this: No one knows exactly when "the(ir) time" is. This poem supposes that an individual, perhaps even a child, believing himself to be perfectly healthy retires from his routine daily activities, confident of awaking the next morning to resume his routine. However, things did not work out quite as planned. Instead of awakening to the sound of his alarm clock the next day, this young person wakes up later that same night staring into the all-knowing, all-discerning, spirit-piercing eyes of God, the Almighty one.

He is now at the judgment seat awaiting tearfully and frightfully his final judgment—awaiting carefully and nervously. He is uncertain as to whether his final destination will be heaven or hell. And so tearfully, he awaits God's final judgment on his life. With tears streaming and memory rolling and his heart now finally and truly repentant, he incessantly implores the Almighty One for just one more chance to get it right. Suddenly the majestic and faithful voice of the Creator of all things speaks to the spirit of the individual, and this is what he says:)

My child, why have you so much to say now that
    you are at the judgment seat?
But you were so quite an unseen when you
    walked among the sinners on earth's streets.

Why did you not say to the sinner, "Turn, you
  wicked man. Turn away from your sins!"
Why did you not tell the liar and the thief what
  was required of them to make it
here *and* to make it in?

According to your own words, why did you not
  minister and evangelize?
And why did you not give an offering and choose
  to rob Me in the giving of tithes?

Why did you not go into the hedges and the
  byways and compel the lost to come and seek
  My face?
Now here you are, incomplete in My assignment
  to you, yet asking Me for mercy and for
  grace.

But what, child, is your excuse for not fulfilling
my anointing upon your life?
What was so important, so meaningful, that you
would make such a senseless sacrifice?

What, dear child, is the reason? And what is your
justifiable excuse?
Am I not to whole you to my divine standards
because of your peer pressure or rebelliousness
or your youthful desire to be amused?

For what good reason did you turn your back on
me and rebel against My very anointing and
Holy Ghost?
What is so powerful and compelling to you
that between My Word, my love, and my
promises, you would love it most?

Say nothing. Rest your heart. Incline your ear.
  And listen to Me as you never have before.
Because what I'm about to tell you will explain
  why some are cast away from My sight and
  some allowed to enter through My doors.

Many, many years ago, I, even I God, took the
  dust of the land,
and I shaped it in my own image, into my
  crowning creation, and I called him man.

Then with the care of a mother nursing a
  newborn babe
I squeezed his nostrils and into that body of clay
  I gave

Life, strength, health, redemption, power, and
  divine authority;
But more importantly, in that lump of clay, I
  gave man all I had . . . I gave him *Me*!

With just one blow into man I blew My power and My might.
In him I blew control over the sun by day and the moon by night!

I didn't just blow air into man's face and up his nose,
In him I blew the Holy Spirit which to me makes him more precious than silver or gold.

In him I blew love that would not in his sisters and brothers seek to find fault.
I blew a level of spiritual integrity that would bring any sin and temptation from Satan to a screeching halt!

I blew faith that was strong, irreversible, and could never die
I blew truth that was too pure to ever tell a lie.

I blew strength that made every man a warrior
and a flesh-and-blood god who was fit and
ready to fight

I blew incorruptible wisdom into his free will
that would only choose to do what was
right.

I blew compassion that made all men love every
other person as if he or she were you

I blew a divine belief into the soul of man that
made him know that was nothing he could
not do.

I blew love and patience and long-suffering and
meekness into every cell of man's clay body!

I blew all of this into each of you . . . because
when I blew . . . I blew into you . . . *me*!

And because it was me that I blew into your
nostrils and ultimately into your spirit man
My very presence in you was your assurance to
cry out, "Come what may, I know I can!"

But the devil came along and told you you
weren't really special—just an image of me.
But when I made you in my likeness, I made you
in the likeness of the entire Trinity.

But you listened and believed the prince of
deception and the father of all lies
And now you stand before me begging for grace
and mercy. Child, dry your weeping eyes.

Listen further because in your vernacular, this
will blow your mind.
Then you will better understand why I God am
not moved by your sorrow or your crying.

There is no reason for any man to run an
   incomplete spiritual race.
Listen to me, child, why I make this case.

I gave you Me and because I am within you
Let Me remind you of only things you ever had
   to do.

First remember, the battle is not yours . . . It's
   Mine anyway!
All you had to do was to yield your members
   over to Me each day.
You didn't need any praise or recognition or any
   fancy fanfare.
All you have to do was to hand the battle over to
   Me and I would have fought it from there.

You can never win this battle on your own power
   or by your own might
That is why I have chosen man's yielded human
   vessel through which my anointing can fight.

Alone? You thought you were in this battle just the one of you?

Even so! A single prayed-up saint can put one thousand demons to flight. In my Word did I not say that is what you could do?

Fear? A spirit not from Me but directly from the pit of hell

Which comes to bring doubt into the hearts of believers and convince them that in spite of having, Me they are going to fail!

But how can you? Do you not know that you know that you know that I am God, the Alpha and the Omega, the beginning and the end?

Who can stand against Me who was around before the beginning and who has already triumphed over every evil and sin?

Child, when I blew into you, you didn't receive just power and permission and my divine authority;

But truly I say unto your spirit man, when I blew into you I gave you . . . M*e*!

I am your rock, your sword, and your shield.
I am your wheel in the middle of a wheel.

I am your battle-ax, your honor, and righteousness and the strength of your life!
I, Jehovah, am your pride and joy, your redemption and the glory that adorns paradise.

I am your peace and passion and the reason you sing and pray;
I am your Lord of lords, the author of your fate, and he who numbers your days!

I am the architect who drew the heavens and the
divine electrician who wired the sky!
I am the great I am and the ageless perfected
faith that cannot change nor die.

I am your Jehovah, your Majesty, your Lord and
God above every other idol god that was or
shall be.
And I am all of this is in you . . . because I gave
you *me*!

I cannot fail. And I do not lie.
I have hidden the rewards of the faithful behind
my curtain I call the sky.

I am God and He alone who creates all things by
the sheer might of my speech.
I am He who knows the secret things of your
heart and he who knows why you fail to
glorify me on earth's streets.

Your faith was weak—too weak to believe that in
that one simple breath
I breathe into your life divine prosperity and an
imaginable level of success!

And because it's Me that you have in the very pit
of your soul
You can speak to the sick and they must be made
whole.

You can tread upon serpents and stomp on the
devil's head;
You can recover the sight of the blind and even
raise those who are dead.

You can speak to the mountains of problems and
tell them to be thou removed and be cast into
the sea.
You can do the impossible because it's not you
doing it. It's Me!

But you didn't receive it. Acknowledge it or speak it into your life.

And because you didn't, you, my child, have made the ultimate sacrifice.

You may not dwell in heaven with the angels, the saints, and the holy trinity.

You may not enter my pearly gates you unfaithful ambassador. Now depart from me.

To dwell eternally in a place that is hot—seven times hotter than hot!

And not because I do not love you, but because I gave you Me but you received me not.

The Heart of Man

(The spirit man—it's an inside job)

Our heart is the center of who we are.

There is nothing about us that is more
precious to God than our heart.

Our heart is our personal throne upon which
we and we alone invite God to sit and reign

Over every aspect of our being.

Our praise emanates from our heart.

Our forgiving flows from our heart.

Our obedience is governed by
the condition of our heart.

Our worship is simply an expression of
the spiritual condition of our heart.

Our prayers are no more than the
communication of our heart with our Lord.

It is our heart which allows us to be connected
to and commune with the Divine.

It is no wonder God teaches us, "Above all
else, guard your heart with all diligence."

A Prayer for Bible Teachers

(My prayer before teaching)

God, we pray that hearts everywhere be touched, set free, enlightened, and made powerful weapons against the kingdom and the power of darkness as a result of what You, through Your Holy Spirit, will reveal to us here today. We touch and agree with the powers of heaven on behalf of every weak saint, every embattled warrior for the kingdom of light, every adversely affected believer, every fragile-minded Christian, and every feeble and challenged laborer for righteousness.

We bind all powers, principalities, rulers of the darkness, and evil desires and motives that seek to intercept and discredit the truth of this teaching and to change it into a message of despair, unbelief, impossibility, and faithlessness. We release a spirit of faith and the warring spirit of our angel Michael himself as our predecessor who will go forth before this word to prepare a pathway that this Word may not be met with hindrance, retardation, trepidation, disbelief, or resistance.

Anoint every syllable of every word that every utterance may be that and only that which You have authorized your teacher to speak and your student to receive in their hearts to encapsulate, retain, apply, and walk therein. Teach us now, Holy Spirit as we prepare ourselves for the smorgasbord of your wisdom and enlightenment. Guide us that we may follow You and never lose sight of and obedience to Your ways.

Speak to us, and we your sheep will hear, receive, and obey Your voice. Comfort us that we will never know fear. Embrace us that we may feel Your loving presence. Console us that we may know that weeping may endure for a night, but Your joy comes in the morning. Commune with us that we may learn You deeper, more intimately, and more truly than we have ever before.

Share with us the deeper revelations of Yourself that we may come to see and experience You in ways and on occasions that we previously never imagined or believed possible. Prepare our hearts now for Your Word and let every believer consciously decide that in your life-giving, yolk-destroying Word will he or she will continue until death or until the rapture. This petition we submit in unwavering faith, having prayed what we have first believed. In the matchless and all-powerful name of Jesus our Christ, amen.

Our Daily Bread

(A prayer to begin our day)

God, our creator and sustainer, we humbly ask that you bless us to see and hear you this day as we go along our way as we never have before. We pray that our eyes and our hearts be opened and prepared as only your spirit can and will do for us. We ask that you remove every binding spirit from every crevice of our mind. We bind every demon and power and principality that would seek to interfere with the free flowing and receiving of your infinite wisdom this day. We curse every evil power, thought, intent, purpose, or demonic force that will seek to bring doubt, confusion, or distrust in you, your Word, or our fellow servant of the light today.

Enlighten us as we proceed to grow closer to you and be more like you. We seek to release the you that is within each of us. Empower us. Guide us. Teach us. Be with us as we seek to come into your presence and be with you at a level at which we have never experienced you, your presence, your power, your touch, or your being before. You are our divine chef. Now we pray that this day you will serve and feed us abundantly the meal of your Word and wisdom that you have prepared for us since the foundation of the earth. Overflow us with the spiritually abundant caloric meal of your wonderful Gospel and truth. We are open and ready to receive your servings right now. Pour, this day, onto and into us until we can take no more. Then, Father, cease not to feed our starving palates with your deliciously wonderful daily bread. Rather, overflow us that we may impart even from our overflow into the spirit man of others today.

We love you and release ourselves unto you right now as we posture our hearts as did Mary at your feet, as we too know that this position is all that is needful in order that we might be highly used by you this day. Secure us in and by your grace and strengthen us to better fight the good fight of faith and allow us in all that we do to never abandon our quest of pressing toward the mark of the higher calling in you this day.

It is in the almighty name of the Jesus the Christ we pray, amen.

The Power of Your Belief

(A child recognizes the need to believe in himself)

How can I do what I dare not believe
How can I become what I fear to conceive

How do I soar as an eagle in the sky
Unless I first believe that I too was created to fly

How can I ever become the god kind of man I
was created to be
If I do not first believe that being so is my divine
destiny

Yet I know I am great and am divinely pregnant
with endless possibilities
But none of them I can manifest in my life until
I have first firmly believed

Believe in myself as a person of godly purpose
    and kingdom destiny
Believe in myself as a force who changes the lives
    of those who come near me

Believe in my spiritual skills which are God given
    and are my supernatural power tools
Believe that I through Him can help others to
    never be defeated, but to always rule

Believe!
Believe!

Open your eyes and see yourself
And love the sight that you see
It is then that you'll come to know
Whatever you can conceive that you can also *be*

A Faithful Spirit

(A mother teaches some of the provisions
of faith to her daughter)

Faith will teach what the intellect can never
learn

Faith will love like no natural mother ever could

Faith will comfort beyond the touch of any
person

Faith will embrace more securely than friends or
family

Faith will guide more accurately than any map
or satellite GPS

Faith will accompany better than any friend

Faith will care deeper than any human heart

Faith will forgive more willingly than any friend

Faith will hear what your words are unable to say

Faith will see clearly that which man's eyes cannot behold

Faith will know your darkest secrets and love you anyway

Faith will cause it to rain upon your desert of pain and despair

Faith will always illuminate your darkest path

Faith will instruct you even as you sleep

Faith will shelter, embrace, and keep you at all times

Faith will forsake you never but abide with you always

Faith will give you God's perfect peace

Faith will bring you in possession of divine
   wisdom
Faith will replace pain with joy and frowns with
   smiles
Faith will . . . if you know it . . . faith will . . . if
   you believe it . . . faith will . . . if you let it
   Faith will
Be ye faithful unto death . . . because faith
   forever will

The Peace of God

(A young girl's troubled soul finally understands
and recognizes the true meaning of peace)

Peace is a special gift from God
It is designed to soothe the soul
To reassure the mind
To comfort to the body
And to embrace the spirit

Peace is God's silent voice
Speaking to our keenly attuned hearts

It is by peace, coupled with faith
That we are able to put doubt on the run
Dismantle confusion, reject hatred
Sidestep temptation and commit our lives to Christ

It is this peace which the spirit needs in order
To operate as it has been instructed by God

Peace carpets our valley floors. It paints the
    ceiling of heaven
And even quails the mighty seas

Divinely given peace is beyond comprehension.
It is beyond understanding. It is beyond this
    earth

Peace is a gift from God to our souls

My Hurt

(A young man's subliminal confession
to his family during dinner)

I'm hurting, but no one seems to care.

It seems so . . . unfair . . . that my family would
let me bear

All of this pain I feel alone and without coming
to my aid

What kind of folks must they be, stupid or
afraid?

They never asked about my grades or why I
refuse to eat

They never ask why I'm always quiet or notice
that I never sleep

They never see depression written all over my face

They never notice the tears in my eyes after
something as simple as the grace

They never notice how irritable and detached my
mannerisms always are
They never notice how much weight I've lost or
that I'm always staring afar
They never notice how I nearly never smile
They never consider last year I ran cross country,
this year I can't even run a mile

They never notice that my piggy bank no longer
stays filled with change
They never notice how illogical I am at times,
almost as if I'm psychologically deranged
They never noticed the excuses I come up with
for all my failures and misdeeds
But let me leave just one vegetable on my plate
and a bushel of admonishment they would
heave

You see, it's not important to me that they notice
    all of these things I've said
But to notice none makes the consciousness of
    one simply beg
To know how can my family not look at me and
    see
The hurt, the pain, and the poorly disguised
    agony
That walks side by side each day with me
And should be as visible as the branches of a tree

How can they not see the pain clearly etched
    upon this face
Desperately imploring their help to please make
    this place
Home again . . . home . . . home sweet home
And to let the practices of drug be long since
    gone

For the hope and will are sincere and are here

But what I need most is the strength I draw from
you, family so dear

That it waters my faith seed with each correction
and tear

It gives me the courage to go on and to face my
fear

Of any obstacle, trial, and even the very toughest
tribulation

I have no doubt because you are my
confidence . . . my jubilation

Can't you hear me? Can you hear the pleas of my
heart?

Begging for you to help me to start

Anew, refreshed, and revived

Loved by you, revered, and alive

All these things and more we can do
If only I can make this point to you
I have succumbed to drugs and am strung out
    strong
I'm sorry I did this, and I know it was wrong

But now more than ever I need a rescue
You have to forget what I did and think about
    what we've now have to do.
I need youall . . . family . . . I need youall to
    stand by me
But for starters tonight, I just need youall to look
    at me and see

Someone who gave you all the clearest signs
Of a loved one desperately seeking help for a long
    time
An innocent child seduced by wicked deception
    and a compelling lie
Who is entrapped by the wiles of the flesh and
    sentenced there to die

I need you to see what my world has become
I need you to feel the pulse of my heart as it
   drums
I need you to hear the words of this mole
I need you to resurrect the life of my soul

I am hurting but no one seems to care
Please don't talk to me about right or wrong, just
   or fair
Don't let me bear all this pain rejected, desperate
   and alone
I need you family . . . to help guide my weakened
   soul back home

To the Women I Love

(The unseen heroes)

To all the very special women in my life
My grandmother, mother, sisters, daughter,
 nieces, granddaughters and wife
I extend love and appreciation to each one of you
And cherish you dearly for all the countless
 things you do

You are the true bond that binds us together with
 sound family ties
You are the feminine gender and the tolerant ones
 who know when my peaceful smile belies
My hurt, my pain, my disappointment, and even
 my deepest desire
Yet you are all my confidence and motivation to
 remain ever inspired

You are the comforters who relieve my pain and
distress
You are my assurance that I can withstand life's
most vicious tests
You are my peace during my internal secret
battles and deepest strife
You are the reason I can rebound and again face
the uncertainties of this life

You are all special to me in your own unique and
loving ways
I pray God's graces be upon you this and all your
blessed days

The Anatomy of a Female

(A salute to our ladies. Written in 1976)

The feminine gender
What a delightfully unique and satisfying
  experience
With a total anatomy of three—sugar, spice, and
  everything nice
You have adorned the earth with your grace,
  beauty, and charm

Your role is often misconstrued and seldom really
  understood
Your thoughts are suppressed and your emotions
  bottled more times than vented

The world has sought to stigmatize your sex, categorize your efforts, and minimize your potential

Yet with the valor of a knight in shining armor, gallantly you have fought on

So seldom are you adequately recognized for your indispensable contributions to a world chaosed by constant mutiny

Science fiction has lessened the impact of childbirth

Technology has diminished your role as a housewife

Yet vast competition, mounting insecurities, and confusion among members of the opposite Gender have frequently forced you to single-handedly undertake the complex role of parenthood

But life goes on, and with the arrival of each new
day, you become more and more proficient
at Disguising tears with smiles and replacing
despair with hope

You were created by the hands of God and
ordained keeper of man
Your tasks have been many, your rewards few
Striving forever, ceasing never, you have
convinced disbelieving chauvinists that the
feminine Gender is that gleaming beacon of
hope in this dark and desperate world

Mama, Can We Talk?

(A lonely and ignored child privately rehearses a planned plea to his mother upon her expected arrival home.)

Mama, can we talk?

We don't have to just sit here.
We can listen to music or crochet or go for a walk.
Or play a game . . . or even pity pat.
You know, maybe we could do something while we talk . . .
Something really, really simple, Mama. Something simple like that.
Most of all, Mama, I just need to talk,
Whether we crochet or pity pat or take a rain check on the walk.

It ain't got to be no long talk, no lecture, or no
  fussing,
And Lord knows, Mama, I don't need no yelling
  or no cussing.
All I want to do is just, here and now, sit and
  talk
'Cause there are so many things that need to be
  brought
Up between us so we can say what we see and
  what we really feel
And finally learn how to talk with each other
  and how to deal
With all this stuff life's just throwing in my face!
Lord, I need to talk to you, Mama, before I let
  go and disgrace
Your perfect name and your impeccable
  reputation
And I'm trying hard not to, Mama, but I need
  your concern and cooperation.

Every day the world seems to just keep closing
    in on me

Showing me all the terrible things I don't even
    want to see.

Sex and the rape and prostitution and crime,

Whoremongering and killing and young folks
    happy to be doing jail time.

A national budget that's completely out of
    control,

Preachers ministering to congregations themselves
    with wickedly corrupt souls.

An educational system that has fallen from the
    world's grace,

People so full of hate that they forgot we all
    belong to the same human race.

Children defying all authority while parents are
    fighting with their own kids,

Women sleeping with women while men are
    wearing high heels, fake nails, and wigs.

Now I know this is boring and you probably
    don't want to listen,
But I wish you would 'cause it feels so much like
    I'm fixing
To explode and just blow up and do all kinds of
    stupidity that is just plain lame!
Some of them I understand but the rest I need
    you to explain.

But if you give me five minutes just to share with
    you what's on my mind,
Then maybe you and I can put our heads
    together and combined
We can lick this thing that's bothering me so and
    eating away at my last gut,
Come on, Mama, talk to me! Give me some help!
    I don't want to fight this thing with luck!

What is there to talk about you look like you
want to ask.
Well, let's see now, Mama. Let's see if we can
unsort this mass.

Well . . . again . . . there are drugs and
pregnancies and aids and gangs,
And violence and incest and abuse and world
leaders who are insane;
There are fears, thoughts, and prejudices and
never-ending strife.
There are cults and easy money and subliminal
messages saying take your own life.
There's TV and guns and politics and war,
And the hate groups who have taken the Fifth
Amendment way too far.
There is religion and science and aliens from
outer space, and Lord knows there's still a
whole lot to be said about the human race.

I truly don't care where your interest lies

I just want to talk so that we can take the time
to get inside

Of one another's minds and one another's souls

And find out what it takes for us to help make
and keep one another whole.

I need to talk, Mama. I need to talk to . . . no . . .
with you

It's a terrible thing, Mama, you don't seem to
need to talk to me too.

Mother's Day 1995

(Written from the perspective of a busy daughter)

Dear Mom,

You just wouldn't believe all the things I've got
to do.
The tasks are so many, the hours are so few.
There is washing and cooking and vacuuming
the floors;
There are feuding children (over who will take
the dog outdoors).
There are ball games and school plays and
concerts at the hall,
There are music lessons and PTA meetings and
huge sales at the mall.

My dear husband is sick and cannot leave the
bed.
"Honey, where's the remote?" for two full days is
all he's said.
Trevor, that cat, never stops chasing our pitiful
parakeet,
Cute little Mikey still paints the wall every time
he eats.

Geoffrey finally reached teenhood and so did all
of his ideas.
Of course, this enlightenment only added to my
parental anxieties and fears.
Money is always tight and, naturally, the kids are
a very picky about what they eat.
And why do kids never hear a thing you say
unless you repeat and repeat?

I once took for granted all of the motherly things
    you did,
I just regarded them as everyday tasks—you
    know, nothing big.
But then I grew up, married, and gave birth to
    my own.
Now I wonder why didn't I listen more when I
    was at home.

Circumstances call so as usual I must go.
But before I do there is one thing I want you to
    know.
Of all the women to ever grace God's wonderful
    earth
I am thoroughly delighted he chose you to give
    me birth.

Happy Mother's Day, Mom!

My Spiritual Mother

(That which is born of the flesh is flesh and
that which is born of the spirit is spirit)

In our lives there often exists a unique kind of
    void

Which can only be filled by a special person and
    Jesus our Lord.

We don't always know the reasons such a void
    exists in our lives,

Only that it does and its presence serves only to
    re-emphasize

The will of Him whose work I so desperately
    want to do

And obedience to His Word to which I long to
    hold true.

Voids are passages impassable except with the
help of another,
Be that helper and a friend, a stranger, a father or
a mother.
Voids are deeper and wider and more powerful
than many know.
They are like leeches that grab on and then
refuse to let go.

Many voids did I know in my private life and
even in my soul
Until you breeched my painful passage and
sought to give me back control
Of my thoughts, my feelings, my emotions, my
spirit, and my life.
Slowly you removed my void with the precision
of a surgeon with a spiritual life.

You took me in like a child born of your very
own flesh.

You taught me to let go and love and how to
bind duress.

You anesthetized doubt and extracted yesterday's
agonizing pains.

You woke up my confidence, esteem, and faith
and now I'll never be the same.

You dared to cross the void which separated me
from Christ.

You gave me your hand and navigated me back
to spiritual life.

You came to my rescue when I was down and
could go no further.

And because you did, in my heart forever you are
my spiritual mother.

My Ebony Mother

(Though barely recorded in most history
books, they are due great honor)

To my ebony mother, giver of life to all humanity
and the legacy bearer for all African and
human roots,

Who was born of shaded hue and suited in an
attire of oppression and affliction, I thank
you.

To my ebony mother who spoke with the wisdom
of the scholar,

Led with the fervor of a warrior and conquered
with the glory of an emperor, I thank you.

To my ebony mother who was later captured and bound and ripped apart from the roots of her heritage and forced to give companionship to the lust and dementia of the masters' erotic desires for her blackened skin, I thank you.

To my ebony mother who allowed the taking of her virtues, the abuse of her sacred body and the discrediting of all of her gallantly bold efforts and accomplishments that she might shield her offsprings from the torment of future atrocities, I thank you.

To my ebony mother who prayed long and languishing prayers in order to escape the consciouslessness of the masters' whips, only to be subjected to the deliberate inhumane blows of the masters' corrupt system, I thank you.

To my ebony mother who proudly braved the armed and hooded forces that sought to destroy my will, deny my dreams, and repeal my dignity, I thank you.

To all my ebony mothers, with global span and timeless recall, I thank you.
For your sacrifices . . .
For your efforts . . .
For your love . . .
For your strength . . .
For your beauty . . .
For your soul . . .
For your insights . . .
For your foresight . . .
For your gallantry . . .
For your backbreaking days . . .
For your lonely and prayerful nights . . .
I thank you.

Oh queens of life and governess of all humanity, I thank you.

Ebony Queen

(A salute to the mother of humanity)

I am an ebony queen.
I am beautiful, firm, smooth, and black.
I give meaning to the mystery of the sunrise,
And am the human wisdom which makes much
of lack.

I am history's guide through many treacherous
ordeals.
I am the wings of angels and the harvests of
many fields.
I ferry your prayers to a divine ear light-years
beyond the sky.
I'm the answer to your conundrum and the
riddle which asks "Why?"

I paraded through time before records were ever
kept.
I was just at the creation and the big bang and
was with Aristotle and Socrates and even
Jesus when he wept.

I have seen all the beauty eternity has spread
before my eyes.
I have orchestrated both joyful reunions and
tearful good-byes.

Yet I am strong and wise and shall never ever
yield my faith!
For in the back of this African queen lies the
strength of her race!

I am the mother of life as predestined by the
Divine.
I am earth's bio-vessel of knowledge and its
sentry of time.

I was created man's helpmeet and alongside him
took my place.
I have honored his divine charge and have
birthed through his seed a human race.

I am an ebony queen,
Youthful, strong, and black in hue.

I am God's gift to all wondrous things.
I am God's gift to you.

A Mother's Love

(There's nothing like it!)

There is no love on earth quite like a mother's
It's stronger than a father's, sweeter than a sister's,
    and more protective than a brother's
A mother's love can soothe the hurt of any pain
    away
It brings bright smiles to an otherwise dreary
    day
It knows no hurt, no shame, no ill feelings, or
    reservations
It only knows mother and child, regardless of the
    situation
It's patient and kind and understanding and
    meek
It's stern and unrelenting and sometimes
    bittersweet
It never ever vacations or even stops to rest

It simply remains constant, refusing to diminish
or digress

It's as powerful as the world's strongest nuclear
blast

And without it, the morality of our children is
crippled and cannot last

It's a keeper, a teacher, a mentor, and a friend

It's a parent's permanent record that's played over
and over from within

It's a gentle touch, a loving word, and an
approving stare

It's what makes mother and child lifetime
partners, an inseparable pair

It isn't just physical and is neither a feeling nor
inexplicable intuition

A mother's love is a state nurtured into existence
by sincerity and proper spiritual conditions

I'm so glad in his infinite wisdom God could see

That in order for me to have all of this I needed
you as my mommy

Happy Birthday, Mom

(My favorite lady in all the world)

Time and events come and go.
Over the years emotions ebb and flow.
Memories are made and then misplaced in time;
But it is for eternity that I shall call you a favorite
love of mine.

You dried my tears when I was too innocent and
helpless to do the same.
You calmed my fears and gave me peace when
the world seemed mean and insane.
You love me all the ways I never knew how and
that only a mother can.
Were it not for the love of you, Mom, I could
never have become a complete man.

Sunday school and church were your standing
weekend rules.
Never once did you waver, never once did you
lose.
Altruism and character were the traits you said
everyone needs.
So you taught them not to buy a book but by
your daily steadfast lead.

Kindness and honesty endeared you to many
who shared your path
Some marveled at your tenacity, I at your ability
to laugh.
Always mindful of developing me into a "God
kind of man,"
You said, "Claim the victory during the battle"
and "Never be afraid to take a stand."

Many years have long since passed, but the
memories seem just as new.

Even today your inspiring guidance remains in
all I say and all I do.

Now I find myself lecturing to my children with
wisdom learned from you

And hoping that by the grace of God my efforts
will be as successful too.

You are the epitome of what every mother should
be.

You are all of the Eve God created before she ate
from the tree.

Mother, I have said all of this just to ultimately
say

I love and thank you, Mom, and wish you a
happy birthday.

Who's My Mother?

Mother is a strange term.

It doesn't always mean the one who gives birth.

Sometimes it means the one who listens,

The one who talks,

The one who guides,

The one who loves,

The one who touches,

The one who teaches,

The one who reaches,

The one who cries,

The one who smiles,

The one who nurtures,

The one who inspires,

The one who disciplines,

The one who relents,

The one who holds fast,

The one who prays,

The one who punishes,

The one who believes,

The one who gives births to dreams.

Are you my mother?

To Grandmom

Grandma,

You have seen and lived through so much more than words can ever identify and mere memory can recall. You've had enough disappointments and pains in your life to share with everyone whom you meet and still retain more than your own fair share.

Regardless of this, you still rise each challenging morning and muster the energy, the love, and the willpower to force through the difficulties of more trials and uncertainties just to make life better and happier for me. And though I don't always act as if I notice it, today, Mother's Day, I just want to acknowledge to you that I do see and appreciate all that you do for me each day. Truly, I love you for more than I can ever say. So please accept this praise as a tiny representation of my sincere and deeply felt gratitude, admiration, and love for you.

God bless you. Heaven smile upon you, and I will always love you, Grandma.

Grandma

(Through the eyes of a young grand child)

Grandma,

When I think of all you do
and all the situations you've seen me through,
my heart goes out and my soul swells with grace
that God sent you to make this world a better
place.

Encouragement to a Spiritual Sister

My sister,

God has any innumerable methods by which he works. He uses these myriad of methodologies to draw us, protect us, purge us, deliver us, promote us, and even bless us. None of us has the right to question his methods, although we all know his divine motive, which is to draw us unto himself. Ironically, when we think that we are being *tested* or *tried*, we are actually (in many instances) simply being used and delivered. Herein is one of the beauties of God. He delivers us from things that we ourselves do not even know are binding us. He sees and hears what we cannot, and He knows what we do not. He understands what we cannot. Thus, he often moves on our behalf and does for us that which we have no idea that he's doing, and even if we did, we are still unable to perform it in our lives on our own behalf.

Often flaws exist within us, but they are so deeply and deceptively concealed that not even we ourselves recognize their existence and operation in our lives. God, however, does. And because He does, he knows what flaws will prevent us from getting to the place where he can release us into the fullness of our callings. Therefore, he reveals those aspects of our character that do not reflect, resemble, or project him. Sometimes it is painful. Sometimes it is embarrassing. Sometimes it results in being alone. Other times it may mean that people will speak harshly about you. But ultimately, that which was deposited in you for the purpose of destroying your walk with God will be purged by God himself for the purpose of purifying you unto himself, his will, and his purpose for your life.

Stand fast in the liberty of Christ. Have no doubt about who you are. Don't sway under pressure. Don't doubt just because of your attack. Rather, be ye steadfast, unmovable, always abounding in the Word of God. Now is the time for believers to be as faithful as we will ever be. Grab hold of God. How do you do that? Get in his Word. Read his Word. Believe and receive his Word, even if you don't understand it all. Just take God at face value. He doesn't fail. He doesn't falter. He doesn't lie. He won't deceive. And he won't leave (you).

There is a Scripture that says, "Do not be afraid when fear suddenly comes upon you." Receive the power and wisdom of this verse. Fear is a spirit ("I have not given you the spirit of fear, but of . . . power and a sound mind.") that is sent from hell to hold our faith hostage. But one with a sound mind (the mind of Christ) will believe, receive, profess, confess, and walk out in his/her life *only* what the Word of God has said.

You are a mighty woman of God, my sister. The devil has to throw every trick in the book he can come up with at you because he knows that once you come into the full understanding and revelation of who you *actually are in the spirit realm,* you are going to give hell and every demon it releases in your path a run for their money.

I pray that you will make the following confession over every aspect of your life:

God, I am your child. I am your property. I am here to serve your purpose. My life is no longer mine but yours. My will is only to do the will of him who sent me. I will only be strong, obedient, and unafraid. I shall never be deterred from professing you as the God of my all. Everything I am, you designed me to be. Everything I will become, you will lead me into being. My eternity is with you in heaven. My vocal cords are yours to command. My feet are yours to guide. My emotions are yours to control. My thoughts are yours, Master. I praise you simply for your majesty and power. There is none like you. I am blessed and complete in you. I am powerful and anointed in you. I am secured and protected in you. And so are my family and my entire household. I will receive your report and your report only. I bless you. I glorify you. I reverence you. I long for you. I worship you. And I surrender all that I am to you and to you alone. Forever blessed are you and all those you call sons and daughters, of which I am one. In the name of Jesus, I thank you. I believe you. I receive you. I am in you . . . and you in me. We, Father, are one. Amen. Amen and amen.

Now receive this and go about your business in Holy Ghost-inspired confidence and *be* blessed. Remember, being blessed means speaking, thinking, and doing *blessed* things and nothing else. Stay in constant communication with God. He's working on you in a way that you can't even imagine . . . and He says "I have heard the petitions of her heart."

Agape love to you and the household.

Your brother in Christ

Random Thoughts

God! Where have you been and why did you stay
so long

I have been empty, scared, and weak since you've
been gone

My faith became weak and my prayer life thin

I began to think that the only way I could
command your presence was to return to sin

I was afraid and uncertain and thought you'd left
me here all alone

It never donned on me that you were simply
preparing me a place to call my heavenly
home

Every time I feel as if I have nothing to smile
about, I immediately think about the things
I could be crying about right now were it not
for the glory of God.

Of all that I was, am, or shall ever be, I am most
happy to be a child of God's.

Every day I awaken, I know that I am great.
I do not seek to find greatness.
I search for no definition of it.
I look to no other man or woman to personify
greatness for me.
Rather, I gaze upon myself and behold greatness.
I reflect upon myself, my skills, my thoughts,
my morals, my beliefs, my faith, my soul, my
Desires, and what I was created to do in the
divine and flawless will of God
And know that if I just do that, I am great.

When I gaze upon the starry sky and imagine
the number of angelic eyes staring back at
me, I am simply awestruck.

Time is not a distance.

Time is not space.

Time is a course every man is given at birth to
travel.

Every man's time is different.

Every man's course is different.

No man is never late or early.

He is simply on time in accordance with "his
time" schedule.

He never arrives or leaves a station along his
travel before or after "his time" assigns him
to do so.

And despite his will, he cannot or will accomplish
any more or any less than has been assigned
to "his time" course;

For God knew he who would vigorously pursue the offerings of *his time course* before he designated and assigned such courses.

Each course has been errorlessly plotted and assigned for the purpose of ultimately manifesting a pure and perfect will that is inconceivable to the minds of men which are *late* in their recognition, acceptance, and reverence of the Almighty.

Some habits are not as bad as they sound. After all, just think what the world would be like if more of us learned how to *lie* (in the arms of Jesus), *cheat* (Satan out of the victories he fights so hard to deny us), and *steal* (away a few minutes each day to spend with Christ).

Who is able to achieve beyond his own faith?
What sighted person can see clearly in the pit of
    midnight?
Who can hear in a chamber of muteness?
Who can proceed while standing still?
Who can behold greatness while examining only
    his own faults?

I'm so glad angels are real. Otherwise, you never
    would have been a part of my life.
Since all skills are of God
Whereforth comes our arrogance?

Since all successes are His gifts to us,
Why, then, do we boast?
Since He has created all things and given place,
    purpose, and time to them,
Why do we seek to receive the praise?
Since He is God and we are man
Why do we desire the worship of others?

If God were more like me
How, then, would heaven be?

*I Love Getting High on
God's Drugs*

Love,

Salvation and

Deliverance

Remembering You

From tricycles to training wheels to showing off
    bullfrogs for screams
From soccer to tee ball to crying over scary
    dreams
From bruises and scrapes to warm campfires and
    by vicarious dates
You are the one who saw perfection in me despite
    all of my mistakes

From newspaper routes and early Saturday
    morning cartoons
From private moments on the phone to being
    restricted to my room
From summer camps and team socials to nervous
    dates and first kisses
You're the one who said keep track of the hits
    and never mind the misses

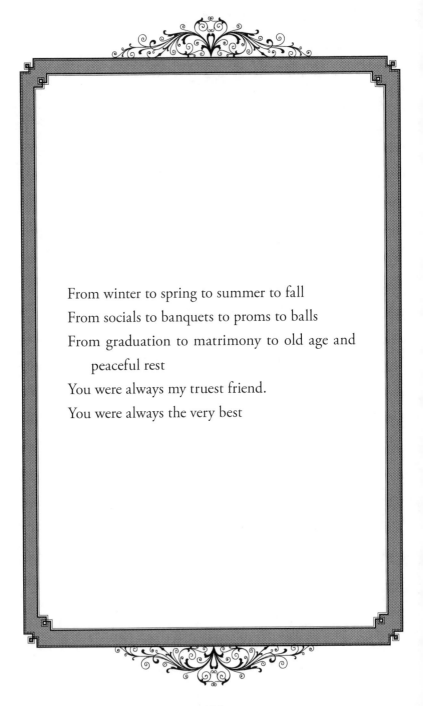

From winter to spring to summer to fall

From socials to banquets to proms to balls

From graduation to matrimony to old age and
    peaceful rest

You were always my truest friend.

You were always the very best

I Do Not Love You
Because I Have To . . .
I Love You Simply
Because My Heart
Chooses To

On Being One

(To My Wife)

I love you now that I know me more

Because I can see what I never saw before.

I see your beauty, grace, and charm

And realize the true pleasure of you in my arms.

I know your heart and understand your words.

I see the invisible and listen to the unheard.

I believe in your smile and know well your soul

Because I am you and you are me and together
we are whole.

Looking For Me

(A teenager searches for and finally finds himself)

Big, bad, brave, and bold
Eyes of steel and a heart that's ice cold.
Thoughts like those of a young delinquent fool
Dreaming of conquering without knowing what
    it means to rule.

Aimlessly, hopelessly searching for "me";
Trying desperately to see what this world would
    let me see.
People and places, attitudes and faces, and love
    and hate, and people of all races;
Evil and good and life and death
Life at its worse, life at its best.

Orphans and families and rabbis and priests
Flowers blooming in tranquil spring while people
 killing like raging beasts.

Stillborn babies and dope addicts smoking
 crack,
Some people being chauffeured and sleeping in
 mansions
Some folks walking and sleeping in shacks.

Welfare and tax fraud and deceit by elected
 leaders,
Food stamps and delinquent youths and example
 setting fathers who are cheaters.

Astronauts and junkies, explores beneath the sea
The world let me see them all, but it couldn't let
 me see me.

NBA, Internet, Facebbok, MMA and HBO too
The conflicting worlds of old school and the one
of technology anew.

Smiles and dreams and aspirations for success
Youths constantly striving, old men at rest.

Pain and guilt and mayhem and strife
Love and compassion and a distorted view of a
happy life.

Rocks and trees and canyons and air
Babies having babies before they can even
compare

Life and death, abyss and the sea
The world showed me all of this, but it never
showed me *me*.

Until I look into myself and summon the glories
of my soul
And learn that I am deserving of life and not the
emotional existence of a mole.
Until I strive and try and succeed and fail
And learn that to get to *me* could mean going
through hell.

Until I laugh and cry and force myself to see
inside
So that I could unearth the *me* that so badly
wants to hide

From the pain and the scares of the events of
time
From the drudgery of my past and the shame
within my mind

Until I no longer run away believing I can flee
The one thing I can never outrun and that thing
    is me.

Until I can accept this challenge and force life to
    show me the *me*
I have never before been able to see

Then I know I can nor will ever be
That which I wish to become most and that is
    me.

But now I know why the world could never show
    me *me.*
Because only I am me and only I can let me see.

For my worth and beauty are not in history nor
    in the time not yet seen.
They are with me here and now and have been
    given to me by the Supreme.

So I will look deep into my soul and bellow out
    my name
I won't run from fear or hurt nor hide my face
    from shame

For I am *me* and about that I will never again lie.
I am simply a product of all things that have
    passed me by.

I hold no wand to refute the misfortunes of the past,
But I do have the powers to change tomorrow
    and to make it last.

So out I come to dwell among those of real life
To seek true bliss and to end the sacrifice!

Off comes the mask! Down comes the façade!
Oh! What a world! See me and guide me, dear
    God!

Look out world, here comes *me*!
By the way, my friend, is the world leading you, see?

Love Is

(Love Must Be Shown)

The ability to accept

The ability to forgive

The ability to pardon

The ability to believe

The ability to hope

The ability to embrace

The ability to laugh

The ability rejoice

The ability to cry

The ability to feel

The ability to understand

The ability to share

The ability to listen

The ability to persist

The ability to touch

But never the ability to avenge

In the Morning

Early in the morning when I rise
I peer through my window and see God outside.
I see Him in the sun, the trees, the animals, and
    even the dew;
And then I hear His voice asking, "But can
    others see Me in you?"

I talk with Him as I prepare for my day.
My soul receives the answers He sends my way.
His words are tender, loving, kind, and sweet;
Then again He asks, "How so you speak to those
    whom you meet?"

He is always encouraging, never vindictive or
mad.
He is wise beyond understanding, yet humble as
a lad.
He knows the earth is His and the fullness
therein
But He doesn't boast, rather, He asks, "When did
you last help a stranger or a friend?"

He's so strong, yet meek and mild.
I start my day off with a cup of coffee,
He starts His with a smile.
I hurry off to work and bid Him adieu.
Again He reminds me, "I'm God, My child,
wherever you are, there I will be too."

Making a Champion

(A motivational poem for middle school
students and teachers)

Champions are not always born—sometimes
  they are made
Through trials, dedication, successes, and even
  dismal days.
They don't always stand aloft with glistening
  trophies gaily held high,
Sometimes they laugh in victory; sometimes, in
  defeat, they sulk and cry.

But never does a champion recoil from the
demands of an earnest try.

For to accept the challenges of life is their answer
to the eternal question why.

They never give up, nor do they even think of
giving in

Because champions know that just to accept the
challenge is more important than either the
loss of the win!

Champions, a rare breed, are made up of
uniquely uncommon stuff;

And though beautiful outside, inside they are
dynamite tough.

Inside a champion are zest, drive, zeal, and spirit
  beyond expectations
While outside they are scholars and leaders and
  people of character and impeccable
Reputations.

Champions know well of the art of introspection
  and digging deep down in their own souls.
Equally as well, they know the tenacity and
  fortitude it takes to achieve both individual
  and Team goals.

Champions never quit, stop, give up, give out, or
  give in
Because as champions, they know that winners
  never quit and quitters never win.
They are strong in virtues, true in faith, and
  regard fear as a sin.
They believe if a task can be mastered, they sure
  are the ones who can.

Champions are not always born; very often they are made.

Being a champion is up to you. It comes down to courage and discipline or simply being Afraid.

Children are champions, over and over and through and through.

But not because they were born champions, but because they were made to be champions by people like me and you.

Success

I didn't know love until I was forced to face the
 world's hate

I didn't know perfection until someone pointed
 out my every mistake

I didn't know joy until I was forced to dry my
 own tears

I never truly knew time until I recounted my
 wasted years

I never knew pleasure until I sat and spoke with
 gloom

I never knew hunger into the movie and together
 we share the small room

I never knew abandonment until I was made to
 stand alone

I never knew loneliness until I had no earthly
 place to call my home

But through it all I never blinked nor deserted
my immovable faith
I inventoried my strengths, packed them up, and
put myself back in the race
I would not quit just because things weren't as I
wished them to be
I became more determined and refused to accept
anything less than an absolute victory

Life has its quirks and turns and at times deals us
all tough hands to play
But the game isn't over just because all you have
left are a deuce and a tray
Many miracles have happened that have changed
the course of history and just in the nick of
time
So you see, winning and losing are not in the
hand you're dealt, but they're in your heart
and mind

Letting Go

(A prayer for a high school graduate)

May God bless you as you go on your way

May His countenance be with you throughout
each day

May His grace and love shield and protect your
soul

May God's kindness consume you and keep you
whole

I pray that His spirit would touch and brighten
your path

I pray that His salvation will forgive your past

I pray that His will becomes the direction in
your life

I pray that God will protect you from evil and
strife

I wish you so much wisdom in all of your
thoughts
I wish you understanding and good counsel and
all of your talks
I wish you peace and compassion from all whom
you meet
I wish spiritual prosperity to all whom you greet

I know that God will never leave you alone
I know we all have sinned but He forgives all
wrong
I know He sees all that we are and everything we
shall ever be
I know obedience to His Word is the key to
blissful eternity

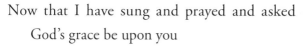

Now that I have sung and prayed and asked
  God's grace be upon you
Now that I have released you to go into the world
  a child anew
Now that I have petitioned unto God for His
  divine protection
Now I release you unto Him alone who can keep
  you unto perfection

My Prayer

Lord, you teach me
And then I will know

You guide me, Father
And surely I will go

You touch me
And I will be made clean

You hold me
And my whole life will be serene

You speak, Jesus
And I will say only what is right

You comfort me
And I will have no lonely nights

You provide for me
And never shall I want or need

You save me, Lord
And I shall be saved indeed

Say Thank You

Say thank you . . . Even when the days of
dark . . . Say thank you.

Say thank you . . . When it seems trials will never
part . . . Say thank you.

Say thank you . . . When all is awry and nothing
goes right . . . Say thank you.

Say thank you . . . Because God has it all in his
hand and He sees far beyond your sight . . .
Just say thank you.

The Lord Is

Lord God you are
>   too good to be explained
>   too wise to be compared to the most sane
>   too fair to ever do wrong
>   too mighty to never be strong
>   too kind to ever be mean
>   too knowledgeable to let anything go unseen

Lord God you are
>   the very reason I can smile
>   the glory in walking every step of every mile
>   the joy and the real purpose in my humble life
>   the only reason I try so hard to sacrifice

Lord God you are

    my everlasting hope instead of despair

    my unconditional support and constant care

    my unquenchable faith and perfect guiding
        light

    my comforter in the middle of a long dark
        night

Lord God you are

    my Rose of Sharon and my Prince of Peace

    my tranquility in the valley, my sun rise in
        the East

    my rain upon my desert and even the food
        I eat

    my guardian angel when I lie down to sleep

Lord God you are

    my protector that makes Satan shudder and
        flee

    Lord God you are everything, everything to me

A Christmas Prayer

Because it's Christmas and all about You,
Dear Christ, hear this prayer and to every word
hold us true.

Let us not be as King Herod and the blinded
warriors of his army
But let our hearts and souls feel and receive what
our eyes cannot see.

May we know that though You were born a
millennium ago,
You're as much Jesus today as you were the night
you slept on the stable floor.

You have never altered, despite technological, time, and societal changes

You are still the one who masters the universe and divinely rearranges

The chaos and disharmony of hatred and evil-spirited men

Into agape-like love that bonds us all as Godly kin.

You are yet He who speaks to the sun and commands it to rise

As well as He who comforts the soul of a baby who cries.

You are yet and eternally *thee*, Miracle Worker and *thee* Prince of Peace

You are He whose coming was announced by angels and a star in the east.

This and more You are to me every day
Because as an innocent baby You came our way.

You departed your throne, sustained in wisdom,
    glory, and power
Just to come and dwell among us for what seems
    like only hours.

And that not for Your own glory, prestige, or
    recognition
But that You may show forth the Father's glory
    and heal us of all of our afflictions.

And heal us You did just as You continue to do
    so even now today
And even now Your spirit dwells within us to
    lead us along Your way.

Now may we always be mindful and truthful to the words of this simple supplication

So that the hearts of men can celebrate the true meaning of Christmas every day throughout our great nation.

On this Your birthday, we pray, sisters and brother, women and men,

And together we all say happy birthday, baby Jesus, and to Him who reigns supreme . . . amen!

Despair

When hard times befall me
And it seems there is no one there,
I am so glad I have the power
To tell Satan, "I dare not despair."

When my times get rough
And no one seems to care,
I'm so glad I have a faith
That keeps me far from despair.

Ups and downs are parts of life
So I don't grumble nor judge what is fair.
I just looked to the hills for my help
And know I have no need for despair.

So when Satan has sent his best my way
This principle I will always observe and declare:
There is nothing that devil can send to me
That will ever lead me into despair.

A Morning Meditation

We thank You, God, for the love that our minds could never conceive, our vessels could never display, and our voices could never articulate were it not for You. We glorify You for Your faithfulness; we praise You for Your awesomeness, and we exalt You for Your truthfulness. Clearly our Alpha and Omega, God, You are truly worthy to be praised. We submit our wills into the encompassing power of Your will and surrender our ways unto Your directing, which truly is the light unto our path.

We bless You for your patience with us, Your confidence in us and Your shedding of Your grace upon us. Sweeter than the honey of the honeycomb You are in our lives and stronger than any attack or stronghold of the adversary is Your presence in us. We bow down and lie prostrate before Your awesome throne and incline our ears to the wisdom of Your voice.

We relinquish any and all control over every aspect of ourselves except our obedience, which we give freely and not out of coercion. We acknowledge, accept, believe, and give confident voice to You as the only true and living God there was, is or shall ever be. Our faith is a fundamental product and manifestation of the basic truths found in your Holy gospel.

We receive You into our lives as the sole creator of all things and the power which gives will, purpose, guidance, and abilities to each creation as You uphold all things by the power of Your immutable and faithful word. You, the God of all things, are my father and Lord, my savior and redeemer, my kinsman and king, my savior and miracle worker, my path and my light, my joy and my peace, my strength and my shepherd, and the one and only God who sits upon the throne of my heart and the throne of all of glory.

Keep and touch us this day. Let nothing or no one go this day without feeling the mighty and majestic touch of Your divine hand. And may they decide to make it their purpose to be used fully by You for the fulfillment of Your purpose here on earth. Touch fathers, mothers, sons, daughters, homes, businesses, schools, and even prisons. Reveal Yourself to all whom You will, and may their spirit man receive Your unctioning unto a higher peace, a more sure existence, and a perfect eternity.

Rain down Your love and mercy upon our lives that we may be the ambassadors and the kingdom representatives You have predestined before the foundation of the world for us to be. We ask You to bless us not for us, but that we may better represent You and bless others by your powers and wisdom and love that remain resident, yet potent, within us.

Now, by Your power, love and anointing, may this day be the best day of our Christian lives, and yet may it be the worse we will ever have henceforth, as we boldly profess now that each day with You is better than the day before. You are our Lord. You are our strength. You are our wisdom. To You, Majestic One, be all the glory, honor and praise forever and forever and forever and in all things.

Amen.

A Sunday Morning Prayer

It doesn't matter who you are or where you are.
Because prayer is universal and without bounds
or limitations, you, your circumstances, and your
blessing are all contained in this supplication.

I pray that you will come to know yourself as
God does. That you will come to determine your
worth as God has. That you will walk out your
destiny as God intends. I pray that you will never
allow the disappointments of your yesterday to
shackle, shame, and rob you out of your divinely
promised powerful and prosperous tomorrow.
I pray that you will clearly understand that not
just *your* destiny but the destiny of your seed,
is wrapped up and eternally controlled by your

obedience to and compliance with God's word and will for your life.

I pray that you will curse every stronghold of doubt and "I can't do because . . ." that has sought to take up residence in and control of your life, your mind, your deeds, your future and that the manifested power of God's grace, joy, and anointing that is upon you spew forth as a river of living and healing waters from you.

I curse every sickness and foul spirit and power of confusion and destruction that has sought to destroy your relationships and spiritual successes. I bound every principality that has displayed the audacity to confront you, God's child. I decree you saved, sanctified, powerful, and full of the glory and pleasures of your daddy, God.

I release you to walk where you have up to now only dreamed of going. To accomplish what you have in time past only desired. To manifest what you have only previously heard about. You are blessed beyond your own recognition. Receive it, and walk therein. Speak it, and accept no other report to the contrary. Decree a thing in the name of Jesus, and accept its timely and purposeful manifestation on, by and in faith. Just know that before the manifestation comes, trials will show up to see if you are faithful to your faith.

The evil one cannot afford to allow you to easily learn nor truly know who you are in Christ. For once you clearly and truly know this for yourself—not what someone at the church or someone in the family or someone on the job or someone prophesied over you—but once you really know for yourself, you will never pray, sing, shout, rejoice, or even worship the same again. Everything about you will change because you will then know that your Father God not only dwells within you, but that you and he are one. Just as he and his son (Jesus) are one, you too are his child. Why then, would he not be one with you? See you, see him. Know him, know you. He has visited his unspeakable glory and his limitless power not only within you, but upon you and your every righteous deed as well.

Gird up the loins of your mind, and begin to know that you know who you are in Christ that God may use your vessel every minute of every day to manifest himself, his will, and his purpose in the earth realm in any and every way he desires. It is decreed that this prayer be made so in the affairs of your life that your joy may be full and the kingdom of God might be benefitted by your service and that God himself shall be exalted and glorified among all creation, and you, his child, shall rest in his glory and hear him say, "Well done, my good and faithful servant. Well done."

Amen, amen, and amen forever.

Why Come We Be Like We Do?

(An illiterate elderly gentleman questions a
youth while sitting on a park bench.)

Now I know we's done been through a heap and
gots a heap mo' to go
But still it's something deep down inside of me
I's jest a itching to get to know
And it ain't so much 'bout every Negro I see—
truth is may only be talking 'bout a few
But I wants you to think about this jest in case
one of dem few is you.

I want you to thank about all the thangs you say
      and all the ways you be
Then I want you to thank about all you ever
      heard and all the good Lawd done let you see
Den as yo'self—and answer real honest—jest like
      the truth done got stuck to yo' tongue wid
      glue
When you see our folks acting the way they act—
      why come you reckond we be like we do?

Why our boys go 'round making babies jest so
      dey kin tell everybody dey's now a man?
And how come our little girls thank they ain't
      nobody lessen deys holding on to any old
      boy's hand?
And why our chilluns jest so ready to quit and
      give up on dey education and school?
'Cause dey's got to know dat without education
      ain't no job to be had . . . and (y'all young
      girls) not even a no-good man wants a fool!

Why our colored teenagers overpopulate every single prison in the land?

But, Lawd, we keep right on a' killing and robbing jest like we's the descendants of a pure mad man.

And why we keep going around believing 'bout us every thang that darn TV man done said

Well, truth is, I reckon you got to 'cause if you ain't got no education it ain't like you picked up no book and read.

Lit'le chilluns having babies—and babies peddling dope

Mamas standing on street corners hooking while daddies out gitting mo' crack to smoke.

Sons fighting teachers and going to school jest to act a big fool

Trying to show everybody that he the one who rule.

But it's his ignorance dat's in control and he too 'shame to jest say so

So he try to look like a man by acting—what de young'uns call it now?—oh yeah, mancho.

Girls coming to school wid they fancy hairdos,
stylish clothes and designer eye glasses
Den dey goes strutting down the hallway—on
dey way to special education classes.
Babies having babies again and again . . . and all
fo' de sad wrong reasons
But den dey come to know dis too late . . . cause
now a new life is here . . . it's a whole new
season.

Ball parks is active and full every single Sabbath
day
Malls and restaurants got so many of us dey have
to turn some of us away
We shop and buy and pay for all the trinkets our
lil' heart's desire
But tell dem sam folks PTA tonight and I declare
dey'll say "You think I'm going? Hump! You
a liar!

Where is our parents, our leaders, our standards,
and our pride?

Many a black folks done fought, bled, suffered,
and died

So that we may be and do some of the thangs
that our spirit will us to

So how come you reckon dem who take
advantage of dem sacrifices is so few?

I don't know, it baffles me and when I think
about it real hard my brain jest plain hurt

To think about how some of us done went from
favor with God to pure pig waddling dirt!

But like I said, it may not be all of us . . . truth is
jest may be only a few.

Anyhow anytime I see my people acting like dis
I jest have to wonder how come we be like
we do.

Warrior's Prayer

While my life is well and in it so little is wrong,
While my spirit is calm and my will is yet
   strong;
While my path is clear and my soul is tranquil
I just want to thank you for being God in my
   life still.

While the spiritual battles are truced and are at
   rest,
While by grace I stand victorious over Satan's
   tests;
While my heart is pure and by faith spotlessly
   clean
I thank you for yet protecting me from the
   hidden and the seen.

While I have no need to cry a single tear,
And while I refuse to lose my faith to the enemy
of fear;
While temptation has rested and taken a break
in my life
I just want to thank you for your son's holy
sacrifice.

While things are good and my outlook is bright,
While I celebrate my walk in your divine light;
While I am filled with the glory of your holy
kingdom
I want to thank you for where you've brought me
from.

For I know Satan has only paused for only a brief
while;
And soon that old devil will again be after your
child.
But that's okay because on your Word I have
supped
And for the battle I am ready—because now I'm
all prayed up.

In Touch

Lord, as long as I stay in touch with you
It's so easy to know what You'd have me do;
I have no need to ponder, doubt, or fear
For your guidance is always so immediate and
    clear.

You guard my thoughts and control my mind
You monitor my speech and are there all the
    time;
You keep a smile spread across my face
You comfort me always with your reassuring
    grace.

You protect my body and keep my soul
You fight my battles while your hand I hold;
You're the keeper of my destiny and the overseer
of my life
Lord, I don't know where I'd be were it not for
Your son, Jesus Christ.

One thing's for sure I've come to know
And I will boldly state it wherever I go;
The longer I stay in touch with You
The happier I am that You're in touch with me
    too.

The Duties of Love

Those whom I have loved, I have also sought to serve.

I have given all of me to them in order to make them better in some way.

I have endeavored to speak words of kindness to their hearts.

I have sought to caress their wounded spirits.

I have tried to shoulder their burdens.

I have volunteered to listen to their stories of hurt.

I have forgiven their transgressions.

I have not sought to avenge their deceit.

I have walked a mile in their shoes, then carried them another mile when they fell victim to fatigue.

I have counseled them against their iniquities.

I have held their dreams in the palms of my hands.

I have run many a miles for their good unbeknownst to them or any other man.

I have upheld their honor and protected their names.

I have lifted them in prayer to my heavenly father.

I have hoped only for God's graces to rest upon their minds and endeavors.

I have treated them as I wish to be treated.

I have loved them as Christ has love the church.

I have done all of these things for you because I have loved you unconditionally . . . and those whom I have loved, I have sought to serve.

3 . . . 2 . . . 1 . . . Eternity

If I had just three minutes of life remaining and what I did, said, thought, believed, and confessed during those minutes would decide my eternity, would I hold fast to my current beliefs or would they change? Would I continue to speak as I presently do, or would I find myself changing what I say and how I say it? Would my mind wander onto the same topics, desires, and remembrances as it now does, or would I fight to purposefully focus it on different thoughts? Would I continue to believe as I say I believe right now? And would I speak the same words over me, my finality, and eternity as I spoke before facing this situation? Would God become more important? More real? More desirable? Would He become my choice or my criticism? Whom would I call and apologize to? Whom would I forgive? Would I ask for prayer or more stuff and things? Would I gather my most precious and memorable books? Or would I frantically search for my Bible? Would I ask for a pint to drink or a pastor to pray? Would every breath take on a new and more serious meaning? And would every second represent a more pronounced and valuable passage of time? Would I party or repent? Would I cry or rejoice? Would I be fearful or faithful? Would I regret or relish in the victory of my days?

Three minutes. Three minutes from eternity. Three minutes from the gates of heaven or the doors or hell. Three minutes from eternally entering the presence of God or sharing the pit of hell with Satan. Three minutes from uniting with Paul, Joseph, Mark, Jeremiah, Peter, Luke, Isaiah, the angels, and even Christ Himself or with every fallen demon who rose up against the unconquerable powers of the Holy One and was defeated, cast down, and are now the permanent residents of hell. Three minutes. Just enough time for a final praise or pity party. Three minutes. A time limit we will all have someday. What will you do with yours?

Never Apart

Though miles apart and dreams away
You're still so near and more precious every day.

Your essence wakes me each morning like the
rising sun
Your spirit reminds me to catch up to a day that's
already begun.

You tease my mind with the gentleness of your
thoughts
You calm my soul with the remembrance of our
talks.

You're so special . . . even from miles and miles
away
That's why I love you more and more every single
day.

Inspired Love

My child, my children,

I laugh with you because my heart knows the joy
    you are yet to feel,
I touch you because your wounds I seek to heal,
I hold you because your dreams I want to make
    real,
I pray for you so that all your agony God will kill.

I counsel you because your soul I wish to be
    pure,
I chastise you because I seek your very best
    demurely,
I cry with you because your disappointments I
    know for sure,
I encourage you to give you hope that will always
    endure.
I love you because God would have me do so for
    sure.

Surrendering of Process

I'm tired.

I'm lost.

I'm collapsing under the weight of my own righteousness.

I'm confused.

I'm dejected.

I'm wandering aimlessly in the wilderness of my man-made mess.

Burdens, like cascading avalanches, consume my soul and obscure my inner vision

Then leave me blinded and seeking to be excavated by institutional theology and cerebral religious concepts.

Subdued by the tempter without even as much as the slightest knowledge or weakest fight

I became ensnarled by my spiritual myopia and unable to distinguish the dark from the light

But today I surrender all that I have over to You that You may stand guard over it

I trust all that I am and shall ever be into Your hands for safe keeping.

Hear my cry, Oh Lord, and wander not away from this supplication.

Increase my will to submit to Your will.

Increase my sensitivity to Your word and Your voice

Stir up the gift of You that is within me

Remove the scales from my eyes and give life to every word off my tongue

Search and purge me, Father. Strengthen that which is weak and replace that which is worn

Illuminate the dark places and speak unto those areas wherein onlyYour quickening spirit can help

Allow the world to see You in me and me in You as I commit my all into your hands this day and forever.

If I Held Just This Day

If I held just this day in the palm of my hand
I'd take every man's failures and replace each one
    with "I can!"

I'd grant every child one special dream,
And I'd give back to humanity that which has
    been stolen by machines

I'd sponge away hurt and band self-pride and
    frowns
And in the lives of the broken hearted I'd heap
    joy by the mounds

I'd give every mother the desire to love and
    embrace the fruit of her womb
And over her own household the presence of her
    precious virtue would loom

I'd paint the sky with the delicate wings of the
seraphim
And all creations would gladly hallow God's
name and reverently bow before Him

The poor would be exalted and would glorify
God for their newly found success
And the condemned would be forgiven and
exalted as some of heaven's best

All the earth's sick would be cleansed and made
totally well
And the demons of affliction returned to their
kingdom then I'd widen the gulf between
heaven and hell

I'd put night on hold and visit every single
twinkling star
I'd kiss the sun, hug the moon, and walk from
universe to universe—no matter how far

I'd dance on the clouds and sing with each of
    God's angels
I'd tour Paradise and drink living water from
    New Jerusalem's holy well

I'd never cease to praise Him for all that He is
And the joy that being in His perfect presence
    brings would be the only composition of my
    tears.

My youth would be forever preserved and I
    would never die or grow old
For one day with Christ puts all other time on
    hold.

Just one day
Just one day
If I held just today in the palm of my hand

Thank You

I do not have the future in the palm of my
hand,
Nor do I possess any control over the Master's
plan,
But today I have covenant with my Savior to say
Father, I thank You, for whatever comes my
way.

I prefer sunshine and people all with smiling
faces,
Friends with clean hearts and visits all to happy
places
But I won't complain when things don't go as I
pray
Because I am committed to thanking You still
for whatever comes my way.

I prefer that pain and confusion would both pass
    me by
And for my spirit to always soar as an eagle in
    the sky
But I love and trust You dearly and have decided
    to say
Thank You, Master, thank You, for whatever
    comes my way.

Then when my times are good and my head is
    again held high
And my joy is boundless and my blessings are
    nigh
Once again I will give thanks unto You and say
I yet thank You, Father, for whatever You send
    my way.

Insatiable Love

Who can measure the boundlessness of My love
  for you
For who is able to comprehend the depth of My
  heart
Who can assign words to the completeness of My
  wisdom
And who is able to determine the eternal vastness
  of My mercies

What creation can contain the whole of My
  attributes
Or what vessel can alone total My total being
What words of yours can give description to My
  joy
And who is it that can accurately compose My
  zeal on paper

Who is able to give either quantity or quality to
    My thoughts of you
And who among you can set divine destiny and
    purpose to his own course
"Only I," saith God. "As only my infiniteness can
    do justice
To that which lies beyond the finiteness of
    man."

Me

I know what you see when you look at me
But do you know what it is you really see

I know the fashions which impress you and the
    words you like to hear,
But do you know the soul into which your
    natural eyes can never peer

Do you know my heart whose prayers you have
    never heard
Do you know my indomitable spirit which
    cannot be deterred

Do you know my hope which is the very engine
of my soul
Do you know my inspiration which refuses to let
me abandon my life's goals

Do you know my past, my present, and my
future yet to come
Then you don't know me because of these things
I am but the sum

A Talk With Daddy

(A Young Daughter's View of Her Father)

I never really knew what I wanted in a man
Until my father spoke to me and made me
    understand
That first I must realize that I am unique and
    free
And that I am to never compromise my standards
    or my morality

My father said, "Sweetheart, you're as bright and
    capable as any man.
You have the right to fight battles and the
    responsibility to take stands
Remain proud and strong and regardless of what
    you do
Be faithful and confident and to thine own self
    be true

"Leadership," he explained, "is not by gender, class, or position.

Leadership is by courage, action, and personal conviction"

Any man failing to grant you the dignity of these traits

Is clearly a man urging you to pass through failure's gates

"A real man must first seek to learn the inner you

For if he doesn't, he will never understand why you speak, feel, and think as you do

He must know that you are different by nature and designed to be so

He must realize though he's bright there are also things that you know

"He must be accepting of your dreams and never
attempt to deny you your role
For to abandon that which makes you happiest
will only create chaos within your soul
He must know well the destructive differences
between partners and a dictatorship
He must be confident enough to accept
differences yet compassionate enough to
tenderly mend rips

"You were created by God from the very rib of a
man
As his help meet to rule over God's creatures and
land
To give birth and perpetuate God's most prized
creation,
To spread His pure and perfect love through
thanksgiving and exaltation

"Your man must know who you are by your
emotions and your name
But too he must know to whom you belong by
divine claim
He must honor you not just in body, but also in
spirit and in soul
He must be willing to respect your temple and
labor to keep it whole

"When you have truly found one such man
among the swelling mass
You will have found a good man and one whose
love is destined to last
Forever and forever and even beyond heaven's
pearly gate
For this is no ordinary man, my child—this is
your soul mate"

My daddy kissed me gently and softly whispered,
  "Good night"
As he slowly left my room and carefully turned
  down the light.
In the silence of my room, with the light lowly
  dimmed,
I now knew everything I wanted in a man—I
  wanted a man just like him!

In Anticipation

(My Hope)

When all my days are over and done
And I have answered the calls of both burden
and fun
Will I be able to say I know a good race I've run

When all my days are over and done
And I can no longer influence the young on their
outcome
Will I hear my savior say, "My servant, well done"

When all my days are over and done
And I can longer admire God's setting sun
Will I meet Jesus in Paradise with my new life
having just begun

When all my days are over and done
And I have to lie down and forevermore hold my
tongue
Will I sing in the heavenly choir or beat the
divine drums

When all my days are over and done
Will I have countless rewards or none
Will Jesus know me not or will He thank me for
the race I've run

Quitting

(Enduring to the End)

I cannot quit
No matter the task
For my helper teaches me
This too will pass
And then only the will
And the glory of Christ
Will forever rule
And guide my life
While temporal satisfaction
Is sufficient for most
I seek eternal life
With my divine host

Race and God

If God loved only white people
And no other race but white
If He is a God of love
Why, then, would He create the brown, red,
 yellow and black

If God loved only the Jews
And no other race but the Jews;
What, then, would be the gentiles' claim to Him
What, then, would be their heaven-bound dues

If God loved only the red man
And no other race but the Native American
Why, then, would He say, "I will draw all men
 unto Me"
Why, then, for *mankind*, were nails driven
 through His hands

If God loved the Negro alone
And none other but the black race
How could He command us to "Love ye one
another"
How could He make such a case

God loves us all equally and He wishes us all to
know
That bigotry and racism are plots of Satan's
which simply must go
He created a single man in his own image and
from the dirt of the ground
And because He did, He loves the white, the
yellow, the red, the black, and the brown

The Rainbow Station

Somewhere over the rainbow . . . way up high.

Somewhere over the rainbow . . . where even clipped-winged birds still fly.

Somewhere over the rainbow . . . dreams are realized and all fears are forced to die.

Somewhere over that rainbow . . . we're on our way—you and I.

We will be guided by our dreams and governed by our desires.

We will seek success and once we've found it, dance to the tunes of our hearts' lyres.

We will trod many a tough and winding paths and shed many a lonely tear

But we will never quit, for each experience brings the rainbow's end nearer.

Success is not only our goal, but our destiny and our duty too.

Come, journey with us, somewhere over the rainbow . . . where dreams really do come true.

Rising

Rising above the disappointments of time
Rising above the obstacles of human frailties—
    yours and mine.
Rising out of the dust of hurt and shame
I'm rising! Rising! Into a waiting world with
    much to gain!

Rising from the ponds of self-pitying tears
Rising from the depression of repressive years
Rising from the abuses and fallacies of a mis-
    education
I'm rising! Rising! Above my world of indignation!

Rising from heaps and mounds of Jim Crowism and Georgia's red clay

Rising from the blackness of destitution into the dawning of a brighter day

Rising from the womb of a battered youthful mother

I'm rising! Rising! Destined to take God's people one day further!

Second Guessing God

(Your Trust In God Must Be Unconditional)

My body was racked and tortured with pain
So much so that it looked as if even death would
    be a gain
But then I prayed to Dr. Jesus and He came in
    and miraculously fixed my condition
But silly old me, I decided to seek a second
    opinion

Then I heard Him speak to my soul and say,
    "Whose word is better than Mine?
Who is he whom you believe is more fit to heal
    your condition than I the Divine?"

A second opinion you have sought on your
already-healed condition
Then do so, my child, but with this one
admonition

Who is he that is better to heal you whom I have
known even before birth
For who knows more about you and your
condition than I, who created you from the
very dirt of the earth.

Who is she who can better prescribe the remedy
to your earthly ill
Than I who likewise created *her* from Adam's
single rib

I am He who placed the healing balm in the land
of Gilead
I am the surgeon for your wounded spirit, the
peace for your troubled head.

I was all knowing before there were institutions
of education
And My mere word produced and sustains the
wonders of the creations

I know of those things that were before time
immortal ever came to be
I know what minds cannot conceive and
microscopes can never see

It is I who command time to begin then to cease
for eternity
Who then do you ask, my child, to second guess
me

You are not healed because the doctor operates
and declares you well
You are healed because I demand the demons of
affliction to lose you and return to the pit
of hell

I am the Alpha and Omega, the First and the
Last and the only true light
I am the lantern to your path and your guidepost
through depressed nights.

I called Lazarus forth and told the dry bones to
live again
From the womb of a virgin I produced a Savior
for every man

I locked the jaws of lions and caused the whale to
vomit on dry land
I turned a staff into a serpent and held back
Abraham's willing hand

I protected Moses and commissioned Joshua's
burial by angels' hands
I gave sight to the blind and made skeptic ask
what manner of man.

I destroyed Sodom and Gomorrah and with little
fed many until they were filled
I grant peace beyond comprehension and order
the stormy seas to be still.

Out of love I have created you in My image and
for my purpose alone
Who then can you turn to to ask if I am wrong?

I am God Almighty, deserving of faith and
everlasting praise
I am your Creator and He who numbers your
days.

Second guess me if you will but this you will
always know.
If your second opinion differs from mine, with
the first one, then, you should always go.

Stand!

(A group of inner city youths openly confronts
those who often unjustly levy inaccurate stereotypes
against them)

So who told you that I would fail
and that I would never succeed?

Who told you that all I ever end up doing
Was smoking crack and puffing on a blunt of
weed?

Who told you that certain dreams were beyond
my "limited" reach?
And who convinced you that I was created to live
my life like some kind of social or intellectual
leech?

Which one of your fancy, tailor-made suits told
you that somehow I was beneath you?
And which one of the letters behind your name
even suggested that I was incapable of
earning some too?

When you drove past me, did the stereo in your
fancy car tell you that I looked better as a
walker?
Or was it your expertise of the king's language
that conned you into believing that I am not
worth hearing as a talker?

And tell me, was it that darn TV reporter that so
easily convinced you
That a set of housing projects and a welfare check
was all our lives are due.

Tell me. Who told you?

Who told you that one baby after another was all
that would ever come out of me
I'm bigger than baby after baby, but this your
arrogance wouldn't let you see.

I have dreams and goals . . . and I want to finish
school and college and become a doctor too
But for some reason society is convinced that
these accomplishments have been reserved
only for people like *you*.

You look in my eyes but you can never see what's
in my mind, my soul, or my heart!
You just look upon these rags and believe we'll
be better off if somehow all our lives we just
manage to stayed far, far apart.

But who told you this? And why in your heart
have you allowed this to become so?

Who told you that there has to be an upper class
of human beings and a class below?

Who told you this?

Am I not fit for more than just running with a ball?
Am I not fit to answer some of life's other challenges and demanding calls?

Don't get me wrong! Touchdowns and dunks are useful and fine. But then too so are learning about engineering and chemistry and brain surgery and flying.

This is not *all* of me. This is not all I will become.
But you can't see that. Because you can't see where I'm going for looking at where I'm from.

Why do you not get to know me? Can you not love me because I'm different from you?
Would you deny me an opportunity? A future? Because your prejudice unjustifiably mandates you too?

Then it's your own heart that holds you prisoner . . .
and not what anyone has told you.

But in spite of the picture you've already painted
of me
I will succeed
And I'll do it without the aid of a weapon, a
gang, crack, or weed!

I'll rise about my current situation and stand
with a thankful heart and a remembering
head arched to the sky.

Never again doubting myself, my abilities, or my
future
Never again asking doubt-filled questions such as
when, where, or why.

I'll just know that I have been rescued for a
reason that even I may not know
And that I'll still have battles no matter where I go.

But without praises, acceptance, encouragement, money, or fame
I *will* achieve my goals in life and *will not* complain.

For I have been rescued by a power that is far greater than *any* man

And now I know I will make it, come what may, because I have been empowered by God to *stand*!

Good Morning, Fear

(An adolescent's conversation with fear)

I knew it would be hard. There was no doubt about that. I had only acquiescently accepted this challenge because I did not want my friends to see me only as a spineless nerd. I needed their support and acceptance. Having it made it a lot easier for me to continue to accept myself, even though there were times when I was most uncomfortable and unfulfilled with my life.

But how could this ever become a reality in my life when fear, my constant yet unwelcomed companion, consistently whispered words of doubt and confusion in my ear. "You'll never do it," he softly insisted. "Why are you fooling and torturing yourself so? You know you don't fit in with them and that you can never do what all the other kids do! Why, you're going to become the laughing stock of the entire school. And then, just think what a fool you will appear to everyone—even to yourself!"

"Why don't you stop it?" I argued back. "Why won't you go on about your business and just leave me alone? Go! Go! Please just go."

"I can't do that."

"And why not?"

"Because you're my business. It's my job to strip away your optimism and confidence. Did you forget who I was and what it is I do?"

"No I didn't. You're Fear. That's who you are—Fear. And you come to cause people to abandon their dreams and hopes and aspirations. You come to destroy everything that's good."

"R-r-right."

"But why me? Why would you want to do that to me? What have I done to deserve you?"

"Why must you do anything at all? I don't come on the basis of merit. I come on the basis of opportunity. I'm what you may call an equal opportunity destroyer. That is, I take equally as much joy in destroying you as I do in destroying anyone else anywhere else in the world."

"But how did you get here. I didn't call for you."

"In a way, no. But you might say that you're the answer to the call for me that was placed before you were ever born. I came for you because someone else called me into their life before giving birth to you. Therefore, when I entered their life, I automatically had easy access to your life."

"No. I don't believe you."

"Believe as you will or must. But it's true."

"You're crazy. And a liar."

"Oh, yeah? Think about it. Do you know why you find it so easy to hate? Because you are afraid—fearful, meaning full of fear—of what might happen if you love. Do you know why you fight? Because you're fearful of showing compassion. Any idea why you lie? You're fearful of truth. And why is fitting in so important? You're afraid—fearful—of showing others who you really are. I've made you all one big race of xenophobic beings who find it more comfortable and easy to zealously yoke yourselves with me and regard your fellow man trepidly, nefariously, and even mendaciously. Ostensibly, you vilify me, while in practice, inarguably you embrace me as your global genocidal tendencies and berating of your fellow mankind clearly shows."

"No, I'll show you! I will! I will! You'll see! I do this! I'll accomplish this even if it costs me my . . . Oh my gosh. What a ghastly dream!"

This is your local 6:00 p.m. news. The war in the Middle East heats up as this has now officially become the overall deadliest month of the conflict for both American and Afghan soldiers. Two unidentified babies found dead on Seventh and Reynolds. Violent crime wave pushes local homicides to a new limit. Governor of the southwestern state signs legislation to have "illegals" forceably removed from her state. And two transsexuals were found beaten to death. Stay with us for this and more after this break.

Dream? Dare I say, I think not.

Yes, Jesus Loves Me

(God's ability to love us is indescribable)

God, I wonder just how could You love me the way You do.

How could perfection look down upon the stench and wretchedness of an undeserving sinner like me, and through all my mess and errors, still see me and say I yet love you?

How in all my rebelliousness, mistakes, and disobedience could You find me deserving of Your love?

As You heard my blasphemous tongue, observed my wayward acts, and knew the meditations of my sordid heart, how could You still love me?

When my sins were manifested in the form of spikes that pierced Your hands and my destiny in the form of Calvary which held You captive to death, when my forgiveness became innocent blood that streamed from Your side and my thoughts a crown that bloodied Your head, how could You still love me? When after all of this, I yet forsook You for the sinful ways of the deceiver and abandoned all You'd done for me, You still loved me.

But how? How does perfection love that which is replete with faults? How does grace love unthankfulness? How does repentance love rebelliousness? How does truth love a liar? How does love love hate? How does light love darkness? Oh, God! Dear God! Tell me. How can You love me like You do? You've called me, predestined me, ordained me, anointed me, commissioned me, delivered me, and sent me forth. Yet I am chief among those who are unworthy. I have been all that You have instructed me to resist. Yet . . . You still love me. You have sanctified me unto You; You have concentrated this vessel unto good works; You have washed me clean in Your blood and even renamed me by Your grace, but yet I do not understand how You could love me so. Agape! Divine! Heavenly love. Pure. Perfect. Peaceful love. Indescribable. Life-changing, soul-cleansing love. You have shed it abroad in Your heart and in my life. How could You love me as you do? You do so because you are love, and You decided to share Yourself with me for no other reason than You wanted me to know You for what and who You really are. And in spite of all else, you, God, are love. And I thank you for sharing Yourself with me. Love. Hope. Charity. These three abideth always, but the greatest of these is love.

A Moment With Jesus

(The Day Starts with a Moment)

Father, I thought I'd take
Just a moment to say
I love and thank You dearly
For granting me another day
To be with You and give praises
To Your divine name,
To honor Your commandments
Without excuses or blame,
To seek Your guidance and
Submit my spirit into Your hand
To recognize You are the creator
And master of the air, sea, and land,
To give all praises and glory to
You and Your angelic host,
And to truly live the life of a Christian
Filled with Your anointing and Holy Ghost.

(Un)Secret Lovers

Hello, Lover.

I just thought I would get up early, sneak away and meet You here in our secret and sacred place. I am yet to disclose to any of my closest friends our place of meeting or the intimacy of our affairs. I never talk with them about how you make me feel each time you touch me all over with your smoothing hands. Neither do I remind them of the sweetness of Your voice as You whisper the very words I need to hear at the exact moment I need to hear them. I never tell them how You strengthen my weaknesses or relieve me of my distresses. I've never talked with them about how You always give and keep Your solemn word to me or that You never break a single promise made to me (or anyone else). Although it is often on my tongue's tip, I never boast on how You always rise to protect me from the bullies of life and time. And I never discuss with them Your level of unequalled patience and forgiveness. You, God, are truly my total confidence, lover of my soul, keeper of my Spirit, and friend who sticks closer than a brother. And while I haven't talked about You very much, my fiends always know when I've been in Your presence because even when I leave our secret meeting place, You are still with me.

Goodbye, Best Friend

I watch you as you sleep
And give you eternally to God to keep.
My prayers go forth before your soul
Petitioning that as in life, over you, God will
maintain control.

(Never Start a Day Without Acknowledging Christ)

Good Morning, Jesus,

A new day has arrived, bringing with it the uncertainties and challenges of the unknown. But I will face its presentations with chivalry, honor, and faith because I know greater is He that is within me than he that is in all the circumstances of the world.

I have been kept by Your grace, awakened by Your love, spared by Your kindness, safeguarded by Your angels and am full clad in the protection of Your Holy armor.

I will view this day as nothing more than another opportunity to demonstrate my love and devotion to You, Your divine principals, and Your incorruptible ways. I shall not be discouraged or swayed. My thoughts are clear and unconfused and my decision to follow You is unchallengeable.

I will meet all obstacles with faith and fervor and count them all joy—even in the midst of the battle—as I know victory is already and always mine.

I will be of good cheer and a keeper of my brother as You have directed me to. I will remain humble and prayerful throughout the day. I will give all honor and glory to You and seek new ways to be more like You in all I say, see, and do.

Your commandments shall be kept in my heart, spoken by my mouth, and demonstrated by my actions. My mind will remain stayed on You, and may all things resting in my heart be acceptable in Your holy sight.

I will study to show myself approved and will seek to lighten the paths of those who have strayed and are in need of spiritual redirection.

I will glorify You in every way and will never be ashamed to acknowledge You as my Creator, Father, Keeper, Spirit Molder, and God. You are my all and all, and this day I rededicate myself, my speech, my thoughts, my behaviors, my heart, my mind, my soul, and my spirit to You and to You alone.

I shall have no fear as You have not given me a spirit of fear. I will pray for, look for, and expect a miracle from You because I know you are a God of faith and miracles.

I shall abide in Your Word and Your Word in me. And since You are the Word, You too shall be in, with, and upon me throughout this and every day.

This prayer of daily dedication I pray and thank you in advance for Your answer to it as You always hear my prayer, dear God. Amen

Giving Up to God

(God Only Captures Those Who Choose to Surrender to Him)

What does it really mean to surrender to you, God?

What does it really mean to willingly come under the total power, dominion, authority, and guidance of someone other than myself?

If I surrender to You, can I still think my own thoughts?

If I surrender to You, can I still chart my own path?

If I surrender to You, can I still be controlled by my own emotions? History? Traditions?

Can I still manage my own time as I please? Or do I now have any time that is truly mine?

Can I worship as it suits me, or must I now
follow the dictates of him to whom I have
surrendered?

Whose laws am I subject to if I surrender?

Whose statues must I keep?

Whose word must I obey?

If I am surrendered, can I continue to hate? To
lie? To steal? To gossip? To live contrary to
your commands?

If I surrender to You, can my heart still fight
against Your ways?

And must my ears listen only to hear only Your
directing voice? The voice of my only my real
and leading Master?

When I am surrendered, will not prayer leap
from my lips daily? And will not faith
abound in all that I say and do?

Because I have surrendered, I have no will of my
own except to remain in the true will of my
captor.

But because I have surrendered, You now fight for me and care for me and provide me with all the things that I need. For thus is the role of the captor toward his surrendered captive. You are my captor and thus my provider, my peace, my provisions, my protection, my mouthpiece, my hope, and my guide.

I surrender all that I have to You, God. You are my greatest captor ever. Help me to remain surrendered to You at all times and at all costs. For to leave the security of Your captivity is to leave the truest beacon of hope, love, protection, absolute power and total liberty ever. Thank you, God, for choosing me to be Your beloved prisoner of righteousness.

These Feelings I Have

(A Valentine's Day poem)

The feelings are there but you just won't let them
go.
You keep them bottled up and hidden behind
your heart's door.
You tiptoe around them and say they're all gone
away
But when I touch you your body seems to say . . .

Hold me and touch me and love me—all of me
Claim me and take me and be my destiny
Understand me and caress me and love me
through and through
But please, baby, don't leave me . . . because my
heart can't take it if you do.

You tremble when I hold you and become mellow
  like aged wine
You forget all the hurt and the pain and talk
  about only the good times
You squeeze me, tight then close your eyes and
  begin to pray
I put my arm around you and my heart can hear
  yours say . . .

Hold me and touch me and love me—all of me
Claim me and take me and be my destiny
Understand me and caress me and love me
  through and through
But please, baby, don't leave, because you'll break
  my heart if you do.

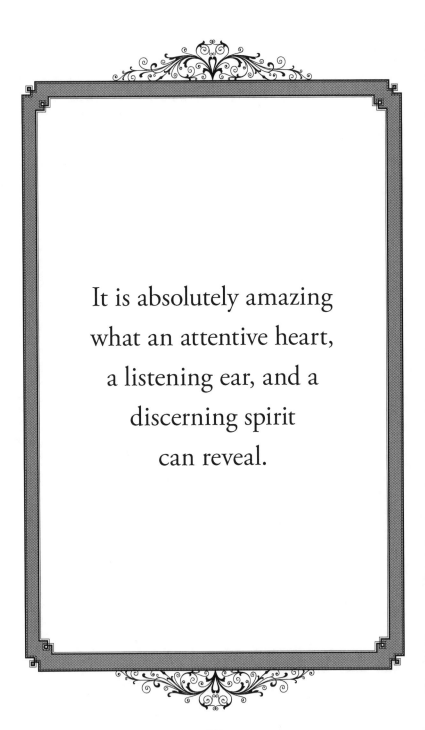

It is absolutely amazing
what an attentive heart,
a listening ear, and a
discerning spirit
can reveal.

Dreams

(You Must Dream Until Even Your Dreams Believe)

I dreamed of one day touching the sky
And washing my face in the morning dew
But someone came and said
That's for someone else. Things like that are not
    for you.

I dreamed of making music and taking
My many beautiful dreams out of my confining
    head
And turning them all into everything I ever
    wanted to be
But someone said that was what someone else
    could achieve
That such a thing was not for me.

I dreamed of being a participant, a winner, a
champion
Someone different and special, someone others
could admire and want to be
But people all around me said, things like that
are done every day.
Then they said they just will never be done by me.

Then I dreamed some more and prayed that God
would send me a miracle
And make all my dreams His dreams. Then I
knew all my dreams I would achieve
And not a single one of my dreams, my hopes,
my aspiration would I ever have to leave
Unrealized, unfulfilled or in some cases even
unconceived
Because as long as my dreams are His dreams, I
could achieve them by His miracles.

I believed in my dreams and in my prayers, and I
    refused to ever let them die
I kept them stored away in the vault of my heart,
    and I saw them every day in my mind's eye.
Because I knew if anybody could turn my
    dreams into my envisioned reality
It would be the miracle-working power of the
    Divine One, who would transform them all
    into my perfect destiny.

As the Cocoon Opens

(All Must Eventually Emerge From the Paralysis of Doubt)

Why can't I?

Why can't I be the person of my dreams?

Why can't I (tomorrow) become that person whom I esteem (today)?

Why can't I own the winners' podium for just *once* in my life?

Why can't I be the victor just one time?

Why can't I?

Why can't I?

Why can't I make my dreams my reality and my
aspirations my environment?

Why can't I be transformed into the very words
of my most fervent prayers?

Why can't I walk the path of success and bliss?

Why can't I?

Why can't I?

Why do I not transcend?

Why do I not obtain?

Why do I not measure up?

Because I have believed the counsel of those who
do not truly *know* me.

I have compromised the essence of *me* that I
might placate the constantly mutable and
jealous hearts of others.

But never again.

No more will I kill me (so) their insecurities may live.

Never again will I lie down so that their weaknesses may stand.

Never again will I remain silent only to become the audience to bold, ignorant utterances.

Never again! Never again!

I am great. I am beautiful. I was designed for success and ordained for prominence.

I have been divinely empowered for undeniable greatness and gifted for uncommon destiny.

Nothing shall in any way deter me from my goal.

I am mission oriented and mission essential.

My life is greater than me and me alone. My giftings are so others will prosper from my presence. My mission has been purposed and is intricately intertwined into the lives of those whom I have been designed to serve.

I am equipped . . . designed . . . created . . . fashioned . . . shaped . . . made . . . and prepared for all that I shall encounter. But it is only my unwavering belief in this mystery that will yield me fail proof and invincible.

I shall never *ever* quit again. And no more will I ask why. But now I will live my life with the full revelation and empowerment of "Why not?"

Why not be great?
Why not obtain?
Why not measure up?
Why not occupy the winners' podium?
Why not become my dreams?
Why not walk the path of bliss and success?

Why? Because I can.

And because I can, why not?

Why . . . not?
Why not?
Why . . . not?

My Daddy

(A Father in the Eyes of his Son)

Who is this man looking at me?
Through whose eyes I will ultimately see,
Myself, the world, and even my own son,
And by whose measures I will someday a man
become.

Who is this man looking at me?
Whose hand I hold in pursuit of my destiny,
In whose footsteps I trod seeking to chart my
own path.
Whose judgment will dictate when to cry and
when to laugh.

Who is this man looking at me?

By whose beliefs I will someday decree,

Whose word to me is as true as God's own grace,

And to reproach his integrity would be an absolute disgrace.

Who is this man looking at me?

Who never tires or reneges on his loyalty,

Who reads me books about fairy tales, places, and oceans,

Who is too committed to ever betray his love and devotion.

Who is this man looking at me?
Who has known all about me since my infancy,
Who teaches me not only society's principles, morals, and truth
But he also teaches me from Genesis, Leviticus, Matthew, and Luke.

Who is this man looking at me?
Who teaches me to look inside myself and see,
The good, the bad, the weak, and the strong,
That which builds mighty men, that which destroys weak homes.

Who is this man looking at me?
Embracing me tightly as he prays on bended knee,
Forgetting never his spiritual maker and king
Never ashamed to honor Him daily as he prays and sings.

Who is this man looking at me?
Who constantly encourages me to be all I can be,
Preparing and striving always to be his best,
Instilling in me the courage to face any test.

Who is this man looking at me?
My inspiration, my guide, and the leader of my
     family,
He's my joy and my glory and I give him to the
     world to see,
The man I love most—my hero—*my very own
     daddy*!

Contemplations

(Written to President George H. Bush upon the inception of the Desert Storm conflict)

When the war is over, and Saddam's threat has
    ceased to be,
And ground troops are needed no more
And there's peace again on the land and sea.

What then, Mr. President, of those who have
    fought brave and true
To ensure the return of Kuwait to those whom it
    is rightfully due?

What then of women and men of color who will
    need your help to secure
Education and opportunities and futures bright
    and sure?

What then of the minorities desperately in need
   of jobs
But only able to find rejection and a feeling of
   being robbed;

Robbed by a government which they have
   proudly fought to represent
In Panama, Grenada, the Middle East, and any
   other place they've been sent.

What then, Mr. President? What do we say
   then?
That America only has a need for their services
   when
There's a war to be fought and an ultimate price
   to be paid?
That we're only concerned about them when
   there's a country to be retaken and land
   mines to be laid?

Or do we peer through the stained glass of civil
   obscurity,
And force our government to act upon the
   injustices we so plainly see?

Do we acknowledge the growing demand for
   additional educational funds?
Or do we forego educating minorities in the
   interest of building more smart bombs?

And minorities . . .

Do we finally gain acceptance for being who we
   are?
Or must we continue to turn off and on our
   ethnocentricity like a flickering star?

A minority in war is not an easy thing to be;
There's a whole lot more to consider than just
   Hussein's Scud missiles and a coalition
   victory.

The thought of returning to the land we call home
Is a contemplation that is neither easy nor
foregone.

The land which says "Go! Brave American! And
fight in the Middle East!"
May well be the same land to cause a warrior's
dreams to cease!

Is this their reward? And have they this honor
earned?
Do they not merit a more fitting prize? Is this
what they fought to learn?

But we are deserving—oh my God, yes!
For the war efforts of minorities are some of the
best!
We too have bled and suffered and died
And fought for freedoms that were denied
To those who were so innocently victimized
By ruthless dictators disguising greed with smiles.

We too are fighters for freedom, as our country
    would have us be;
And we will fight until it comes because we
    believe in liberty!

But then . . .

Will you love us America? And then try to
    understand
That we too take a special pride in this place we
    call our land.
Will you then begin to see
That our most important victory must always be
The one that turns prejudice into love and hatred
    into brotherhood
Just as all our founding fathers prayed that each
    of us would.

Will you then understand how it must feel to
    fight for the riches of Kuwait
Only to have our government return us back to
    the ghettoes of every state?

We don't want handouts or food baskets or
   special privileges or welfare,
We simply want a kinder, gentler government—
   one that's concerned and cares.

One that believes in the abilities of "Little
   Timmy" from California's Watts,
As fervently as it does in a Kennedy or Bush or
   the offspring of a "Senator Cox."

America! America! The greatest land on earth!
I challenge you to love us all and to forge for the
   world to this new birth!
A birth of love and respect and a continual
   commitment to what is right
To providing equal opportunities to Orientals,
   Native Americans, blacks, and whites!
To fight right here—on our own soil and in our
   own government that which we know should
   never be . . .
Prejudice, social injustice, and racial inequality.

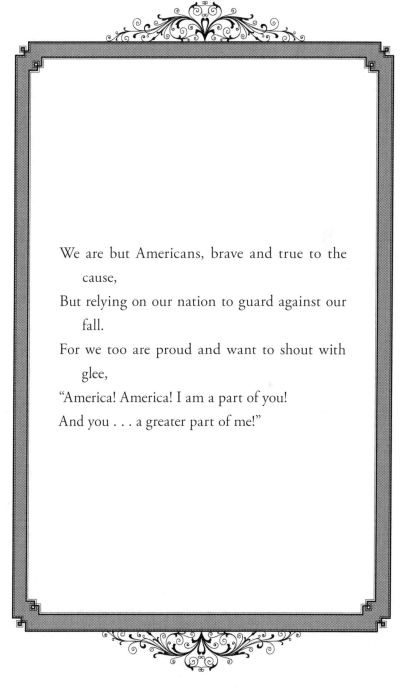

We are but Americans, brave and true to the cause,

But relying on our nation to guard against our fall.

For we too are proud and want to shout with glee,

"America! America! I am a part of you!

And you . . . a greater part of me!"

Come Forth

(A Charge to the Youth of Today)

Children of my people who bled and died
Who smiled behind a mask that often lied
Whose smiles belied frowns and
hid aches and moans
Who prayed that their pains
would soon be gone.
Who prayed to their God with a
faith that never ceased to be
Who in spite of prayer died deaths
of dehumanized agony.

Where are you now? Today?
This moment in time?
Where are you? Can I just one
strong black offspring find?
Where are you? In the home? The
church? On the street? In school?
Or have our forefathers all died only
to benefit a modern-day fool?

The Call to Freedom

(The Effects of Tolerating Abuse)

I heard a bird this morning
And all I could do was cry.
I heard him whimpering
As if he were going to die.

His voice was gentle,
His wings he flapped in pain,
The diminishing sounds of his gentle chirps
Were driving my heart insane.

He was beating and panting
And prancing with an urgency that defied his
    ills,
He saw me watching and peered at me
Through eyes that gave me deep, deep chills.

His chirps of pains and blooded wings
Were offerings to the gods that be.
This divinely adorned feathered creature
Perched in his home of steel was begging to be
  free.

His wings were blooded, his eyes inviting,
His chirps a trumpet to any listening ear
But his soul, oh his soul, how it did fervently
  beg
To have freedom near.

Fatigued and weakened,
Broken and with a spirit that only cried,
This beautiful feathered martyr
Exhaustedly hung his head and died.

We Yet Scribe

(The voice of black history challenges
the youths of today)

King Hannibal, Malcolm X, Dr. King, Rosa
Parks—all made their contributions to
recorded black history.

But now the unwritten pages of our legacy await
to be scripted upon by the likes of you and me.

They beg *not* to keep recording Martin Luther
King's *I Have a Dream* or Malcolm X's *By
Any Means Necessary*

Rather, these unscripted pages of tomorrow's
black history impatiently await to record the
contributions of blacks like you and me.

"Sure!" our history is yelling, "Malcolm was great! King—sterling and beyond words. Harriet—a tremendously courageous warrior. And Hannibal—a fighter, a conqueror, over and over and through and through.

But that's the history and the contributions of *those* individuals! Now on pages yet unwritten, how will I remember *you*?

Will I remember you as a man, a woman, a child of pride, integrity, and destiny?
Or will I record you as a shameful failure? How? How? How will our contributions to *black history* be recorded? You . . . and me?

How? How will we be left on my pages for the next generation to see?

As a woman full of pride and self dignity
Who's not ashamed to proclaim, "I'm here for you
    to look up to and not just lie down with me!"

And my brothers, black history also awaits to
    pen your entries in its inarguable journals of
    infinity.

But *how*? How? How will our history record our
    black men of today? How kindly will black
    history record our present day brothers for
    our future young men to see?

As mere seed droppers? Bed warmers? Baby
    makers? Dream snatchers? Crack cocaine
    hustlers? Jailbirds? And men who have simply
    squandered away much valuable time?

How will black history record your contributions,
    brothers, when tomorrow's young people read
    your biographies, *line by line*?

It's no longer about Malcolm, Martin, Rosa, Hannibal, or beautiful Nefertiti.

Black history of the twenty-first century—the new millennium—will be made by people like you and me.

So make your mark! Do your thing! But whatever you do, do *something*, and know this one thing to be *true*.

Black history is alive and growing and isn't just about what people of the past have done

But also about what people like you and me decide or fail to do.

Back in the days, long before you and I,

From the continent of Africa there went up a great cry

From children, and warriors, and medicine men,
and every royal prince
A cry that pierced the very eardrum of God—
one like which another has never been
bellowed since.

It was *this* cry that told of pain and agony and
defeat and inhumanity to people of dark skin.

It was the cry which signaled the death of
millions of young black children, heartbroken
mothers, and proud fathers who would never
again be regarded as real men.

But wrapped up, contained in, part of that awful
cry that came deep from some nameless black
prayer warrior soul.

Was a proclamation, a promise, a prophetic
dream that someday this broken black race
would be reunited and *would* once again,
someday, be whole.

But now . . . today . . . this moment in time, a diabolical plan to unfold . . . unravel . . . unwind.

And it would not stop this hideously painful process before millions upon millions had bled, prayed, and cried.

This unfolding, unraveling, unwinding, would not stop until over 120 million *black folks* had died.

And their broken spirits, their downtrodden hearts, dashed hopes, and deferred dreams were the only bits of faith onto which they securely held.

As they trod through the blood and the guts of their slaughtered brothers and sisters in order to record their painful stories for black history to someday tell.

And now . . . this day, their story . . . *we*, their uplifted and emancipated ancestors, have come here to majestically proclaim.

And like those warriors, those princes, those inventors, and even those slaves of yesterday, we proudly come alongside their achievements, make more glorious black history and to record *our* contributions and *our* names.

Beauty

The beauty of beauty is not its touch

The beauty of beauty is not its smell

The beauty of beauty is not its value

The beauty of beauty is not its notoriety

The beauty of beauty is not its importance

The beauty of beauty is not its uniqueness

The beauty of beauty is not its color

The beauty of beauty is not its taste or shape

The beauty of beauty is simply . . . its beauty.

A Prayer for Dad

(God Help Our Fathers)

Lord, help my dad to be more like You
in all his ways
So that I can follow his steps
and trust in what he says
Let him be more of a torchlight
in the lives of men
Let him be shelter unto the homeless
and compassion to those needing a friend
Let him love with a spirit that is pure and clean
yet judge no one for judging is left to the Supreme
Let him stand tall in the face of temptation and
    sin
while denying none his counsel be it stranger or
    friend

Let him adhere to the guidance of Your will
while encouraging others to live even stronger
lives still
Let him lead by example and display the faith
that sustains
let him dessert no battle no seek refuge from
spiritual pain
Let him love You and trust You even unto his
very own death
knowing his reward is in passing not merely
taking the test
Being a good father isn't an easy thing to do
but of course You know that because You're a
Father too
So please guide him and keep him and
take total charge of what he becomes
Then I know I'll be just fine because
so goes the father, so goes the son

A Simple Prayer to Begin Your Day

(That I may remember to pray throughout the day)

When God created man, he decreed, "Let us make man after our image and after our likeness and let man have dominion." Significant here is God's declaration that it is *man* who, after his creation, will assume dominion over the earth in God's stead. He (man) was then created in the form (image) of God and was subsequently a partaker of the spiritual powers (likeness) of God when God blew (shared Himself and His divine attributes) Himself into man. This portion of Himself that he imparted into the vessel of dust called man is very important as it is the sole connectivity between the spirit and the physical realms. It is via this *breath* or spirit that our limited spirit contacts, receives, and hears from his unlimited Spirit. Thus was the vehicle of communication between the spirit and natural realm, called prayer, given unto us. Since God will not make himself out to be a liar (by violating His own word of declaration "Let man have dominion"), yet he will never leave nor forsake us. How then does the Good Shepherd act on our behalf if we have dominion in the earth realm? Simple. Since man has dominion, he then has the authority to invite into his world any powers or help or even superior authority he chooses. Prayer is the channel or frequency by which or on which we contact God and legally authorize the Divine and Sovereign One to intervene in our earthly affairs. In other words, prayer is man's natural permission for God's supernatural and divine intervention. Prayer is vital. It is real. But most importantly, prayer is powerful. It is the single most powerful tool we have in our mighty arsenal, and it is strong to the pulling down of strongholds and the destroying of the yokes of the kingdom of darkness. It should never be omitted or taken likely. To not pray is to avail yourself to every attack the adversary throws at you. Prayer is not just your requests made known to God, but it is God's legal right to enter into the earth realm and to fight on your behalf. It is the authority, humility, obedience, and submission He seeks from those who truly need Him, want Him, trusts Him, believe Him, and wish to satisfy Him. There is nothing ritualistic about prayer. It can be done anywhere and at anytime and can last for any length of time. Nonetheless, it is an act that should be performed as many times a day as possible, for God is never too busy, too tired, or too preoccupied with more important things (as we often are) to hear our prayers to him. First Thessalonians 5:17 reminds us that as believers, we are to "pray without ceasing." Below, for those who have not yet developed a strong enough prayer life to discern some of the things we as believers should be praying for, is a prayer that may be read silently or aloud as many times a day as you would like that God make do with you, through you, and for you exactly what he would like—blessings always.

Enlighten us, God. Feed us with the substance of Your holy presence and Your unwavering faith. Allow us to walk upright, pure, and sanctified. Strengthen our every weakness and forgive our transgressions, even if we committed them without knowledge. You have taught us that *all* unrighteousness is sin, not just the unrighteousness we knowingly perform. Wash us with the unmatched truth of Your eternal Word and grant us a peace that is not as this world gives, but only as You are able to give. Let us be convicted, convinced, and converted into a transformed vessel who is fit and willing to proclaim from the depths of our recreated hearts, "It is for God and God alone that I live, and it is for Him and Him alone that I will die. For to live for You is gain, but to die for You is even greater." For if I seek to save my own life, I will lose it; but if I lose my life for You, eternal life with You will be my reward. God, perform on us your kingdom math wherein subtraction brings about increase and division results in exponential multiplication. For the more of ourselves that we allow You to subtract from our own thinking, acting, and being, the greater we become in You, in Your perfect kingdom and in our divine purpose. Thereby do You get greater use out of us, and the greater the use, the more lives we impact; the more lives we impact (dividing ourselves), the more disciples we make; and the more disciples, the more laborers (multiplication). Focus our prayer lives with the intensity and the accuracy of a powerful spiritual laser. Allow the petitions of our prayers to surgically cut through every type, kind and substances of evil, to lighten the world of darkness, to speak to the spirit persons of the deaf, and to remove those spiritually infested and infected areas of individuals who do not know You. Strengthen our every spiritual act and keep us committed to Your laws and statues. Open our spiritual eyes and permit the scales of godly blindness to fall there from that we may see You as we never have before, know You as we have never perceived You, commune with You more regularly and closely than we've ever experienced before, and fellowship with You out of the abundance of Your forgiveness and mercy and our love and devotion. Touch us, God, like and where we have never felt your touch before. Send a shiver of anointing throughout us that we may know that which we have felt in our natural bodies is but a manifestation of the release of Your supernatural powers and presence within us. Bless our thoughts that they may be pure and God sent. Bless our meditations that they may all may be fit for your acceptance. Touch, ordain, inspire, and bless every utterance that proceeds off our tongues that everything that we say shall serve only to bring others into a higher knowledge and a clearer understanding of just how awesome You are and how privileged we are to be blessed enough to even have been predestined to be called Your children. Purge us, God. Purge us as with hyssop. Everything that is not pure and holy and ordained by You and pleasing to You and approved by You, no matter how gratifying to the flesh or the intellect it may seem, we boldly and confidently and obediently rebuke it in the almighty name of Jesus our Christ. Fill us with Your wisdom. Fill us with Your praise. Fill us with Your love.

Fill us with Your forgiveness. Fill us with Your holiness. Fill us with all of the attributes that make You You. You are our peace. You are our strong tower. You are our provider and our provisions. You are our Savior and our keeper. You are our Lily of the Valley and our Rose of Sharon. You are our battle-ax and yet you are our comfort and our comforter. We bless You with the fruit of our lips and the desires of our hearts. We acknowledge that You and You alone are the only God fit or capable to ascend the steps of the universe's throne or to be crowned King of Kings, Lord of Lord, Creator of all and eternal, sovereign, ubiquitous, and all-powerful governor of all things, dominions, powers, and principalities. We are hungry for You, God. We long for You in every aspect of our lives, and as a thirsty deer pants for sacred water in the midst of desert heat, so do our hearts and spirits seek after You in the midst of our earthly trials and our daily lives. Bless our faith that it shall never fail us, for without it, we can never please You. It is by our faith that we contact You, receive You, and obey You. Now, God, keep us in Your holy and securing graces. As Your Word has taught us, Your grace is sufficient to see us through all things. We dare not doubt one word of Your infallible scriptures, for Your gospel is our key and spiritual road map unto You and a blissful eternity. We give You our hearts, minds, souls, and even bodies to keep as your members and vessels for Your use only. We pray that never shall we knowingly permit any member of our vessels to be used for any cause or purpose that does not line up with the teachings of Your word. We pray for Your universal church and every member of it, not just those who will serve it during our lifetimes, but also for those of future generations who will be taught by us but have been ordained to carry forth this gospel after we have fallen asleep and await our spiritual extraction (rapture) from this realm. Bless Your people everywhere, God. Bless them in every country and upon every continent and of every tongue. Bless the poor, as well as the prosperous. Bless the learned, as well as the unschooled. Bless those with infirmities, as well as those who are whole. Bless those who do not yet know You, but have been ordained from their mothers' wombs to serve Your kingdom in this realm. Keep them in the palm of Your hand and by Your love and kindness, we petition You to continue to draw them unto and into You. We praise You and worship You just for Your divinely majestic nature and decree that You are worthy of all the praise, honor, and worship we can give You and more. For if we have ten thousand tongues, we couldn't praise You enough. We commit this petition to You in full confidence that every utterance herein has been heard and divinely met. And so we decree this petition alive, active, and enforceable in our lives as of this very moment, in the name of Jesus, our Christ, we pray. Amen.

Believing God's Word and Prayer

(That I may know my inner man confidently)

It is nothing short of amazing how believers in the Most High God can so easily confess defeat, low self-esteem, contempt, unforgiveness, and lack of compassion for those of less fortune. How can such be? How can one be the "seed" of the One who describes himself as "(God is) love," commands us to "Love ye one another," and admonishes us that it is by this (our continual) love of one toward the other that the world of non-believers will know that we are His children, His offsprings, His ambassadors, His redeemed, His peacekeepers, and His vessels of honor.

How can one who recognizes his true relationship with the Master of All Masters possibly experience low self-esteem? How can one who knows the he is the child of the creator and the sustainer of all things possibly esteem himself lowly in his own mind and heart? How, when and from where has such a thought crept into our thinking? Is a king's child poor? Lacking? Wanting? Needing? Neglected? Without provisions? Without counsel? Without safety? Without support? Does he not have the full force of his father's kingdom and arsenal at his disposal? Does not every asset of the kingdom patiently and obediently await his beckoning summon? Will not his father dispatch even his last emissary on his behalf to grant the desires of his heart? He does not fight. His Father's army fights on his behalf. He does not coward beneath challenges, for he is confident that his Father will exercise his full authority and might to protect, defend, and secure him. He knows no fear, for he knows that it is by his Father's will, permission, direction, and authority that all else exists and is not presently utterly destroyed. His confidence is impregnable and knows not how to wane. He is steadfastly confident in his devotion to all assignments upon which he has been dispatched for he is certain that no force nor authority in all of the cosmos is with the ability to override, overcome, rescind, or refute his father's predestination upon his life. He is committed to the commission that is upon him and the Commissioner who has so ordained it to be. He is blessed, but he is not arrogant. He is wise, yet not "smart" according to the foolish and carnal knowledge of man. He is mighty, although he appears weak. He is humble, yet mighty in faith. He gives, even to those whom others decree as unworthy. He loves, especially those who hate him. And he prays for everyone, particularly those who wrong him. His heart is a reservoir of forgiveness and his memories are void of judgments and the trespasses of others. He smiles during periods when others faint; yet as a watchman upon the wall, he weeps when others rejoice, and he sings songs of praise and thanksgiving during their days of lamentation. He is but a vessel among vessels, chosen and ordained by the Craftsman of Craftsmen and the Potter of Potters, as a vessel of honor and one ordained onto good works among men for the kingdom of light. How, then, can one of such a knowledge see, speak, believe, or receive a report of contrast? Whereforth does the esteem of one in true possession of this revelation diminish to a level that may rightfully be described as "low"? Only one who does not believe the words of this prayer could possibly accept such a report:

Our Father which art in heaven

Hallowed be thy name

Thy kingdom come

Thy will be done

On earth as it is in heaven

Give us this day our daily bread

And forgive us our trespasses

As we forgive those who trespass against us

And lead us not into temptation

But deliver us from evil

For thine is the kingdom

And the power and the glory

Forever and ever and ever. Amen

Purge Me That I May Be Holy

(If a man, therefore, purges himself from these,
he shall be a vessel unto honor, sanctified and meet for
the Master's use, and prepared unto every good work
—2 Peter 2:21.)

It is the Holy Spirit which empowers us to purge our wills, desires, lives, thoughts, words and activities that we may be fit and qualified for use by God. However, we must truly and wholly commit and surrender all that we do Him. We must understand that we must do it His way, as His is the only Holy and righteous way to do it. Surrender and come under the control and power of another that you may forever live free.

God, I thank You that You have shared this tiny, but powerful piece of Yourself with me that I may live wholly, completely and earnestly for You. God, I surrender all of me into Your authority, power and control. Wash me, Father, with the truth and power of Your inerrant and divine word and fill me with Your Holy Spirit that I may better serve You and let my light so shine that men may see You and worship You In that name that is above every name-Jesus the Christ—I pray, praise and receive the words of this prayer. Amen

Hold Fast to Your Confidence

Stand on your faith or you shall not
surely stand at all

God's word is truth and it is my firm conviction
and acceptance of this that gives, grows and
establishes my faith in the reality, accuracy
and the trustwordiness of His word, promises
and prophecies in my life. All about me is a
dazzling mixture of lies and truth, imitation and
authentic, real and fabricated. But through my
faith I will stand, and without it, surely I will
falter, fall and be consumed.

Bless me, God, with your faith, a faith that
neither falters, fears or fails. Increase my faith,
Master, that I might better serve You, serve others
and remain a sanctified vessel. Let not my mind,

my feet, my heart or my will betray Your will or law. Keep me pure and Holy, God. Protect me all the day long, even more so than yesterday. Protect my faith, God, and empower me to be a son in whom You are well pleased. Oh Father of Faith, I humbly submit this supplication in the name of Jesus my Savior, amen.

This Day With You

(The Day You Hear His Voice . . . Decide)

This day I will learn more of Your truth, seek to recognize more of Your glory, speak more of Your power and rely more on the truth of Your every promise. Father, open my eyes, ears, spirit and will that I may see Your eternity in a fleeting second, hear Your wisdom among all of earth's distractions, receive You into the depth of my inner man dn be transformed from a being of worldly knowledge into a vessel of Godly wisdom. Teach me, God, how and when to teach Your people. Anoint me, Father, that I might observe eternity in a second, beauty in that which is intrinsically unappealing, value in that which has been destroyed, strength in humility and purpose in that that many have deemed senseless.

Let not the guile and words of men sway my heart or my path. For You are my daily bread, my water from the well of life, my shelter from storm and my refuge in times of war. Protect me, God. Teach me, Holy Spirit. Shelter me, oh Loving Father, in the security of your all powerful arms. These things are now done in my life because I have not asked amiss and I have asked believing that I already have them. I now call these things which do not exist as though they were and by faith I receive them into my life now. Thank You, God. Thank You, Father. Thank you, Sustainer. Thank You, Creator. In the name of Jesus, my personal Christ and Messiah . . . amen.

Amen to Your Word, Decrees and Promises

(Let Every Believer Say and Stand On <u>AMEN</u>)

Because every fiber of my being stands in perfect and unwavering belief and harmony with Your promises and spoken word over my life, my destiny and my purpose, I surrender my entire vessel into and unto the powers, the laws, the ways, the statues, the promises, the teachings and the reproofs of your inerrant and Holy ways. I pray that I shall never depart from the words of Your divine instructions to mankind. I surrender all that I am back into Your hands that I may be controlled, convicted, converted and convinced by all that Your Spirit reveals unto me. Let me hear Your voice with the ears of my inner man and move ever swiftly along the path of obedience that I might maximize each opportunity presented to me to serve and glorify You. Keep and perfect me as I am unable to do either myself. Yet I receive as absolute truth that it is merely my reasonable sacrifice to render this vessel as a willing and obedient tool of Your kingdom. This, God, is but a joy and a pleasure for me to do. For each time that I do, I not only honor You, but I become a missile of Holiness that has been fired by heaven into the evil camp of the diabolical deceiver. Bless me more and more God, but not for me, but, rather, that I might better, more deeply and ever more powerfully bless You, Your kingdom, Your statues, ways, purposes and power. Cover me, God, with and secure me in the secret place beneath Your impregnable wing of safety. God I pray that You will rock me to sleep with the rhythm of Your angels' voices, oversee me with eyes that never slumber or sleep and awaken me with the touch of mercy which is re-newed every day. I take not a single one of Your promises likely or skeptically, God. I, with full confidence and expectation, stand rooted and grounded in Your impeccable and truthful word. You, God, have spoken, decreed, activated, and caused many supernatural and miraculous powers to reside and operate within and on behalf of me and the Kingdom of Light. I am Your child, God, and until the day that I fall asleep and await the return of my Father, my big brother and the heavenly host, I vow to forever and ever continue to carry on the pre-ordained purpose and ministry of our "peculiar" family. This is my purpose. This is my promise. This is my vow. In the matchless name of Jesus the one and only Christ . . . .

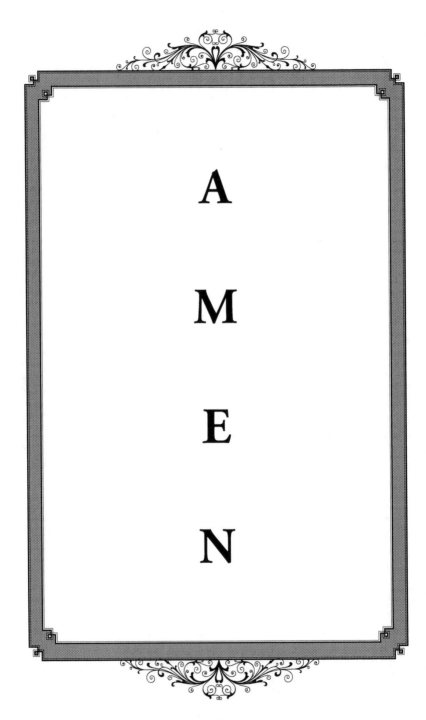

A

M

E

N

Our Generations

Samuel Williams, IV, (son), Jordyn Williams (granddaughter),
Samuel Williams (father and author), Sharleen Williams (wife),
LeAndre Williams (granddaughter) and (seated on the floor)
Shundalynn Williams-Walker, (daughter).